CHURCH MUSIC
TRANSGRESSED

CHURCH MUSIC TRANSGRESSED

Reflections on "Reform"

FRANCIS P. SCHMITT

A Crossroad Book · *The Seabury Press* · New York

For those several generations of Boys Town boys
to whom I owe a great part of my musical education.

1977 · The Seabury Press
815 Second Avenue · New York, N.Y. 10017
Copyright © 1977 by The Seabury Press, Inc.

Library of Congress Cataloging in Publication Data

Schmitt, Francis P
Church music transgressed.
"A crossroad book."
1. Church music—Catholic Church—History and
criticism. I. Title.
ML3007.S36   783'.026'209   77-9424
ISBN 0-8164-0355-4

CONTENTS

FOREWORD
Face the Music

Through no particular fault of mine, that is what I have done: faced the music. As an upperclassman, I had toyed with the idea of becoming a Capuchin friar. Having had a case of something more than puppy love for my Alma Mater, I suppose I wanted the affair to go on forever, but when I was told that as a Capuchin I would be likely to find a place somewhere in a music department, I balked. So what have I been doing all this time? A couple of weeks after my appointment to Boys Town, Father Flanagan asked me whether I thought I could handle his choir while their instructor took his vacation. No harm in that. Except that was in June 1941, and the two weeks turned out to multiply like the loaves and fishes.

Now that everything seems to be winding down, I have no regrets about having faced the music, for the boys always faced it with me. And I have few regrets about having complained publicly during those years that so many who passed for musicians were not themselves squarely facing the music. I only regret—as one regrets the day's discourteous voiding of unfinished dreams—that my Church, literally, does not face the music. There is only one word, a much overworked word, to describe the state of the music of the Church: "incredible."

Church musicians tried in vain to accommodate their music to liturgical reform, not perceiving that it would not be reform they had to deal with but revolution. And revolution is no re-

specter of logic or goodness or beauty or the dicta of authority
—new, old, or passing. Political scientists have pointed out that
revolutionary movement usually follows the Hegelian triad of
thesis, antithesis, and synthesis. The antithetic period has been,
and still is, so devastating and pervasive that I do not expect any
of us to be around for the synthesis when and if it comes. One
has no choice short of madness but to be an optimist; and I am
an optimist of the stripe of Anton Heiller, who remarked to me
recently: "Look, we have always thought of Church music as an
important thing, but it is not the *most* important thing. I am not
concerned about evanescent things like the jazz Masses . . .
perhaps what we think of as Church music will not reappear for
a century or longer."

So there are no guidelines or ready-mix recipes to brighten
these pages. No hurrahs for a corner just turned, no peering at
mirages just over the next hill. There are only reflections on
what was, what is, what might have been.

I should be grossly remiss did I not express my deep gratitude
to Paul Henry Lang, Myron J. Roberts, and Ralph Thibedeau
for their painstaking readings of the manuscript and multiple
suggestions.

∼ I ∼

RETURN OF THE LATIN LITURGY

Quite suddenly, like the tentative patter of a spring shower, one hears of the acceptability of Latin again. Maybe it is because a host of objectors has fled the scene. And maybe it is more like the melancholy splash on fallen autumn leaves, a nostalgia at once hopeful and forlorn. Some complain that the window is now only open a crack or two, but through it whiffs of a Latin liturgy wreathe back in. *Back* is the proper word, for despite the averment of the Constitution on the Sacred Liturgy, it was effectively disavowed by a propaganda that won a new legalism which was often illegal.

One does not speak here of the sad machinations of those who call themselves traditionalists and yet lock themselves in their own version of a Tridentine complex that would admit of no further tradition;[1] nor of the unfortunate Father DePauw, with his oversized ads in the Saturday *Times* and slick come-on brochures; of the Sunday rush of bitter, disillusioned people— so great that the extra traffic police may be a minor contribution to the city's default; or of hard-line rightist groups like Una Voce, which tend to mistake inept language and questionable taste for heresy, and whose pamphleteers are forever talking about the beauty of Gregorian chant, by which, it turns out, they mean *Mass VIII,* a piece neither traditional nor all that beautiful.

Quite apart from the occasional church which has never totally abandoned the Latin, or part-Latin, sung Mass, one discovers small signs of resurgence, usually where there are choirs and young people and students. Even where choirs are being re-formed, not to say reformed, parenthetical Latin motets will surface; upon which happening, pastor, choir, and congregation beam as over an infant's first utterance. In the outport fishing village of Petty Harbor, Newfoundland, the *O Sanctissima* comes through quite as firmly as any other three hymns of the syndrome. There are accounts of Latin Masses at university centers, some as special events, some scheduled regularly as often as twice a week, and some which outdraw the Saturday night "liturgical" campus bash with less claim than it to esotericity. At an episcopal consecration in a midwest abbey, once renowned for its chant, a patriarchal schola is reassembled and sings with reflective aplomb the great *Jubilate* Offertory for the second Sunday after Epiphany. Pick-up choirs which service downtown city churches during Holy Week unabashedly sing Latin settings of what we used to call the "Ordinary."

Even in Rome, the bulletin board in the Hotel Victoria sports a notice of Latin Masses in three fairly offbeat churches: one on Sundays and two on weekdays. And at Christmas 1974, the Holy Father sent a booklet of minimal Latin chants called *Jubilate Deo* to all the bishops of the world, expressing the hope that this might be used as a basis for internationalizing the sung liturgy. While there is no telling how many copies got off chancery office desks, a recent issue of *Notitiae* dressed out a couple of pages with fragments of letters of episcopal approval, including a sa-lute from the Bishop of Greensburg, Pennsylvania. About the same time, it described with approval and thanks the activities of the British Association for the Latin Liturgy, founded "to promote the celebration of the liturgy in Latin in full conformity with the directives of the liturgical renewal." An American asso-ciation of like intent was launched in St. Louis in 1975.

Cui bono? Well, some, The spectacle of a member of the Latin rite preferring Latin appears to drive no liturgical ogre to the wailing wall any more. Left wing puritanism has gone the way of Joe McCarthy. If someone likes what is too glibly called "the Latin mystique" better than "Sesame Street," who's to com-plain? It might be written off as just another vernacular frag-mentation, like the mushrooming liturgies in national parishes.

It is said of Lambert Beauduin[2] that while his life work was prophetic of much of Vatican II, he had a blind spot where the vernacular was concerned. What made him distrust it was the maudlin use to which the vernacular had been put in the German paraliturgies that infiltrated Alsace during and after the First World War. One wonders what he might think of the use to which it has been put today in official liturgies. I think it is more an escape from the maudlin, and not simple nostalgia, that people seek. Still, nostalgia for something good and beautiful will not be gainsaid. Call it a rut, if you will, but the one thing about being in a rut is that you know where you are, and probably where you are going.

Small comfort is derived from the samplings of the still-running apologists who are determined to point up the minimal effect of liturgical experience on the thirty percent drop-off in Mass attendance: But that does not explain the phenomenon of the attraction the liturgy apparently had for Catholic adherents as recently, say, as 1960, when the Vatican stance on birth control and related items was quite the same as now. I do believe a prominent Canadian choirmaster when he tells me, with a degree of simple verity, that the practice of birth control is a contributing cause of the paucity of recruits for his children's choirs, for he is not playing percentages. We needed no poll to tell us that the decline in Mass attendance represented a substantial erosion of faith. What might have been looked into was a kind of reverse application of the old principle of *lex orandi lex credendi*. Do you severely shake, or even just appear to the ordinary man to shake, the *lex orandi* without shaking the *lex credendi* as well? If you don't, and then ask him why he no longer goes to Mass, he will likely excuse himself on the second count, or one of its moral derivatives, though the first is the cause.

Of course, there will be no such thing as the return of the Latin liturgy. It is no use for the pastor to assure his traditionalist callers that they wouldn't know the difference between the old Latin and the new, for they are by now confirmed in their Tridentine heresy. Apart from their accusing Pope Paul of heresy, one wonders why they weren't treated as gingerly as Hans Küng. Even those whom the vernacular has not pleased are past crusading, and there are not many left who have "loved long since and lost awhile." During that while, a whole generation has grown up feeling, unless I misread their native good sense, like so many guinea pigs. One might properly ask the more giddy of their teachers how it is that they account for so large a segment of that thirty percent. Maybe some few of them will find in the subtle wind shift a patch of manna where they had been shown stones, a wellspring from that dry rock. Maybe in their maturity they will learn that, like their Orthodox and Uniate friends, they have organic ties with a civilization that reached sovereign peaks, unaided by management studies or sensitivity sessions.

What have we done with this inheritance? Well, we can say with Christopher Dawson that at least we have *had* it. It is perhaps too late to heed the interventions of a liturgist like Louis Bouyer,[3] who tried to tell us that Our Lord worshiped in a language at least as dead then as Latin is now; or the vexations of Jacques Maritain and Dom Aelred Graham with the elitist tendencies of some liturgists. We need not fail to fault those who, with deliberation and glee, battered and permanently mauled so towering an achievement. And that is not to mutter in traditionalist style Langland's lament in *Piers Plowman:*

> *It seemeth now soothly to the world's sight,*
> *That God's work worketh not, on learned nor on lewd,*
> *But in such manner as Mark meaneth in his Gospel,*
> *If the blind lead the blind, both shall fall into the ditch.*

~II~

THE ART PRINCIPLE

I t is almost ten years to the day that I remarked in closing out my contribution to *Sacred Music:* "In the end, the art of music will have to be met on its own terms if it is ever again to be described as something integral to the act of worship."

The matter of Church music as art, as an integral part of the liturgy, has always been bothersome to me. Not in itself, for there are few propositions I find more readily acceptable, but because the hypothesis always was, on paper if not in fact, that somehow sacred art could, indeed must, go a different route than art in general. The rules for sacred art, it was suggested, came from on high and, unlike its profane counterpart, *ars sacra* could qualify only if its governing terms lay outside itself. No distinction was drawn between the *use* of art and art itself. Its use, not itself, was its end.[1]

This fuzzy thinking, I submit, spawned all that liturgical enfilade about Church music's sole qualitative role being one of function, art or no art. If art itself is not functional, it is time to take a functional walk and stop talking about music.

In any case, there are all those dicta in the Roman documents, from Pius VII to Pius XII,[2] and they are not even given lip service anymore, for the art principle has been effectively abandoned. It is, of course, part and parcel of that vast crusade, perhaps evidenced most clearly in educational circles, against any kind of intellectualism. It is curiously plaited, not with understanding care for the common man but with elemental disdain for him. Perhaps that should not surprise us, for the common man is as uncommon as any intellectual.

If you posit Church music as art, and then say that it is integral to worship, as Pius X did in his *motu proprio,* you are demanding a great deal. The demand has been adjudged unreasonable and unfair, not by plumbers and farmers and housewives, who quite possibly understand and enjoy art, but by unsolicited spokesmen who do not, and who consider that because they are impervious to artistic sensibility, everyone else must be too. So they have kept the principle of integration but denied the art principle. And they have pulled off a larger invasion of amusical forces than Hellebusch[3] ever dreamed of—and this to the accompaniment of a singularly outlandish cry for Catholic composers to meet *their* demand.

Despite widespread opinion to the contrary, great composers were still writing for the Church right up to the 1960s: Kodály, Stravinsky, Křenek, Hindemith, Villa-Lobos. There has been scarcely an Alleluia since. It is true that a man like Penderecki thinks of a particular church setting when he writes a religious piece, measures its acoustics, and prefers its performance there. Early on, most of the competent composers tried their hand at vernacular settings, and some of us commissioned them. But the frequent change of rite and text soon proved this a futile effort. The "final" texts are devoid of that literary substance necessary to inspire any sort of music, which, in the nature of things, stems from the consciousness of the poetic mind. (Aiden Kavanaugh says that they have all the flair of a wet potato chip. This, unfortunately seems to be true, not only of the English ones but of most of those in the West.) And so, only the hacks remain. This may seem a little unfair, for not all of them were always hacks. Forced to build upon present premises, they haven't much choice, if they insist on writing at all.

No one is likely to produce unless he is trusted. And I am afraid that distrust was implicit in all of those high-minded pronunciamentos that we were wont to rely on; that there, in the constant caution against art for art's sake,[4] lay the seeds of the final denigration all about us. Against that unfailing background, it was no problem at all for Helmut Hucke or Joseph Gelineau to damn, up one page and down the other, *l'art pour l'art* quite as much as anything profane in a 1965 volume of *Concilium.*

I have long thought that either the matter should not have been brought up at all or, once brought up, pursued to its philosophic root. For it really wasn't necessary to bring the matter up. Didn't everyone know that once a religious piece was admitted to the liturgy it *had* to be ancillary? But before that, if it was any good at all, it had to be met on its own terms. As Jacques Maritain has observed, "The work [of art] to be made must be an end in itself, an end totally singular and absolutely unique." And Arthur Lourie of musical art: "Melody discloses the nature of the subject from whom it proceeds, and not that of the object"—no matter how earnest the espousal of that object may be. This is not the artist's fault. It is the way God made us. And if we are to offer Him art in worship, it will have to be within the terms He laid down.

One would think that theologians might have sensed the near introcession of art with the divine, recognized it for what it is, as Dante did: the grandchild of God the Father. Archbishop Graber of Regensburg, in a well-wrought discussion of art and religion, put it succinctly:

> There is a causal connection between God's creation and the artist's creativity. In and through the artist, God continues His own creation in this world in His own unique way. The artist can create only by his participation in God's creative power. Therefore his art is really a re-creation of the pattern set in his own soul by the Divine Creator. Thus he serves as God's particular tool whose highest obligation is to present and reveal, somehow, to his fellowman the infinite in finite form, the timeless in the timebound, the permanent in the temporary, the essential in the accidental, the eternal ideas of God in the ephemeral matter of this world. And so the *purpose of all true art lies in art itself*, solely in the freedom of action of the God-given talent.[5]

This was pretty heady stuff for those iconoclasts who called for "a certain daring" necessary to the stripping of the temple. And what they forgot, in their prattle about the Constitution's safeguarding music indigenous to mission lands, was that the culture and art of the West was indigenous to a lot of people too: They forgot the high notion of sacrament, how for aeons "day to day sheweth glory, and night to night uttereth speech."

They forgot that Jesus was the Father's Word and Image, the ultimate redemption of all art, even when it appears satanic.

John Michael Sailer[6] had declared that religion which renounces its alliance with art is either dead or untrue to itself: dead when it has no more drive to expression and expansion, untrue to its own self when it tries to reveal itself without using the essential tools of expression.

It was one thing for the magisterium to insist upon true art, the while holding it up to some suspicion. At least arguments could be made for one position or the other. It is another thing when not the magisterium but almost an entire Church (which lately some tend to confuse with the magisterium) has indeed renounced its alliance with art. Is that religion then dead, as Sailer said? There is a good deal of talk about it. I do not believe it, even if I accepted the specter, in one of Robert Hugh Benson's novels, of a final benediction for a faithful remnant in a dim and secret London apartment at the end of all things. But that in these matters our religion has been untrue to its own self, that it is trying to reveal itself without using the essential tools of expression, there can be little question.

GREGORIAN CHANT

By 1958, Dom Ermin Vitry,[1] sometime secretary to Lambert Beauduin at Mont César, had been promoting and observing liturgical renewal for fifty years. That spring he wrote concerning the chant: "It will be restoration or disaster. May God grant that the chant shall not die a second death, for from the latter it would never revive." He went on to quote a young man who had asked him how it was possible that a people having such a treasury of song could have forfeited it in the first place.

It was not outright, feckless forfeiture, of course, but prior to the laborious restoration late in the last century, there had been an erosion of many centuries. It seems to me that of all the considerable store on the loss side of the ledger since 1958, the bland desertion of that vast body of treasure is the most tragic. The second death was allowed, and swiftly, as if it mattered not at all.

The usual admonition to honor "especially the chant" does not qualify Article 115 of the Constitution on the Sacred Liturgy. "Great importance is to be attached to the teaching and practice of music in seminaries, in the novitiates and houses of studies of religious . . . and also in other Catholic institutions and schools. To impart this instruction, teachers are to be carefully trained and put in charge of the teaching of sacred music." Small matter, for however singular the intention, its execution turns out to be pretty much of a sham. Nobody is in charge of anything, because everybody is. From the dingiest Confraternity of Christian Doctrine conglomerate to the seminary to the

Yale Institute of Sacred Music, Everyman is the planner for a kind of Town Hall Variety Show. It is almost impossible to find a seminary where much importance is attached to the teaching and practice of sacred music.

Article 116 of the Constitution does indeed acknowledge "Gregorian Chant as specially suited to the Roman liturgy; therefore, other things being equal, it should be given pride of place in liturgical services." If, from the perspective of ten years, the language seems cautious, there was no caution in throwing it to the winds, though the conciliar vote on that proposition found only eight or nine in partial disagreement. Apparently other things were a lot more equal. Adrian Nocent and Père Gelineau had been saying that chant wasn't equal all along. I remember my astonishment when I approached a bishop friend, whom I counted a perceptive musician, in a futile attempt to persuade a member of the hierarchy to accept the presidency of the Catholic Church Music Association of America. He thought that, yes, the *Veni Creator* and a few like chant pieces ought to be saved. And my anger at a priest-editor who opined that in any case he would rejoice when chant went the way of the yoyo. That he went the way of the yoyo is perhaps not beside the point.

So neither that *chantelette* called *Jubilate Deo,* nor even the latest generous and noble gesture from Solesmes, the new *Roman Gradual,* is very likely to reinforce Article 116; nor will the going practice in the Roman basilicas of clerks bellowing chant Ordinaries betwixt the wanderings of operatic tenors and basso profundos in realms of ersatz polyphony. Father Vitry was right, as he usually was. It *is* disaster. Not so much for the chant as for the sung liturgy of the Roman rite.

Lest one has not noticed that the opening lines of the tract antedated Vatican II, allow me to regress to the problem that chant was, and to the challenge of it that was never met. It is commonplace to say that the chant was not something tacked on to the liturgy (like the catchall banners whose usefulness no one has yet thought to enhance by cutting them out of flypaper), but that it grew out of it, like mountain flowers breaking through the snow. Not so ordinary was the judgment that chant *as music* was music without peer: witness the insensate effort that was channeled into chant accompaniments after the Restoration. And not rife at all was the notion, expressed by some with no temerity, that the old chants were almost a part of the faith, a vesture giving vision, very life, to the myriad texts of writ they clothed —a kind of scriptual heartbeat.

If one is unwilling to concede any of these three points, there is not much sense in discussing the chant. And it had its professional detractors long before all the pastoral abracadabra afforded them a convenient crutch. These people were not particularly to blame, for either (1) they had native musical blindspots, (2) they had probably been exposed for a long time to inept teaching, or (3) they had been subjected to an unrealistic surfeit of chant by those who used to pontificate that nothing short of chant was worthy of the temple. There certainly was also the tedium of repetitive, often lesser, Ordinaries as opposed to the Propers—the exciting annual excursions through the near-eternal fields of chant's pastoral innards. Or maybe there was too much listening to the chant being mauled by well-meaning but incompetent scholae. This is open to some question, however, now that "Michael Rowed the Boat Ashore" has been dispatched beyond recognition by the Nashville Center, and no one seems to mind.

It is nonetheless curious that when Hollywood was of a mind to insert a piece of chant, say in *Come to the Stable*, or when it intruded into almost any Ginza opera, it became a hit. An enterprising Chicago retailer unloaded a thousand recordings of the Gregorian *Requiem*, having counted on the musical score of *A Man for All Seasons*.

In any case, as I wrote in the last issue of *Caecilia* in 1965, "I am not here concerned with the detractors and professional enemies of the chant: I am mightily concerned about its friends." And a year later, in *Sacred Music:* "Gregorian, Renaissance vocal polyphony, and the rest will become the property of the secular university and the traveling choir, not because they are no longer pertinent to worship, but because erstwhile champions never really understood or cared for them *as music* anyway. They were fads, unsuccessfully perpetrated on the uneducated by the half educated."

I had spent a good part of my bootless editorial life arguing with the friends of chant, often excoriating them, especially if they accused me of fetching fagots when they deemed it not fagot-fetching time. I do not know that I should pursue the same tactic again, but at least we were not then fighting over a cadaver. I had grown weary of being told, in effect, that I must light two candles and bow my head in the presence of the manifold gifts and half-voiced records of Neo-Solesmes;[2] much as I had, probably out of a youthful Franciscan prejudice, shied away from a similar posture before every jot and tittle of St. Thomas in the Louvain-ridden faculty of my favorite seminary.

The infighting centered around attitudes and the age-old problem of Gregorian rhythm. Was it free or measured? Most serious scholars were mensuralists, something which presented no great practical problem, since only rarely did a performance publication bypass the Vatican Press. During the controversy that ensued upon the publication of J. W. A. Vollaerts's "Rhythmic Proportions in Early Medieval Ecclesiastical Chant," Willi Apel noted that while Father Vollaerts had not come up with *the* rhythm of medieval chant, he had given us something much more valuable because it represented an historical reality, that is, the rhythm of MS. Laon 239. The Vatican (and Pothier) had been right, I thought, when it presented its edition in 1905, in opting for a practical compromise, necessary if it were to serve the universal Church.

If, then, the rhythm was to be free, as the Vatican proposed, was it oratorical, or was it hemmed in after all by a kind of Mendelssohnian *un' due tre–un' due* piece of romance? What astonished me, when the fun was all over, was that apparently too many had been more concerned about method, about the intricacies of a system, than about the guts of the matter—a disease common among educationists.

They could have been but lightly brushed by the triple valuation of chant alluded to above. For all that it had suffered a degree of corruption over the centuries, its essential nobility survived, not just in the service of the Church, but as a prodigious generative force in the music of all the West, from des Prés to Duruflé, from Bach (his towering *B-minor Mass* or the *Acceptabis* theme of the *Passacaglia and Fugue,* for example) to Honegger and Janáček. And Gregorian first attracted some of us from out the pages of the old Malines and Ratisbon books.

What might have calmed the rhythmic waters was Lourie's conviction that in the end there could be only angelic melody, "but not an angelic rhythm, because in eternity there is no longer time, but there is and there will ever be praise"[3]

The *coup de grace* was delivered after the Council by friend and foe alike, and curiously, for identical reasons. The crux of the matter was the vernacular, and there the chant caught it from both left and right. Both insisted that with the passing of Latin, Gregorian chant too would be passé. The left had always held the simplistic theory that somehow the problem of Church music was a linguistic not a musical one, and that, given the vernacular, song—the know-how and desire for it—would appear in the land. The right insisted that Gregorian be saved in its Latin home or there would be none. And shortly there was none. My feeling was that it had survived outside that home for nearly 300 years in England, and that in some manner the English experience was worth looking into.

On this side of the Atlantic, people like Leo Sowerby and Ernest White were willing to help.[4] As far back as the 1956 Assisi Conference, where Rome still held to the Latin line, Father Vitry reported that the "crowd was not always well controlled whenever the vernacular was mentioned," and he observed that if the chant were to be saved it would have to be, in some measure, in the vernacular. At his graveside, the chant was in English. Around that time, Père Gelineau was springing his "sprung rhythm." You don't hear much more Gelineau than you do Gregorian now, but it was widely supposed to be the vernacularists' answer to psalming, and it didn't seem to matter much what language it was sung in. Vitry decried the phenomenon on purely musical grounds, but he also quite correctly feared that it might endanger the chance for a resurgence of the Gregorian psalmody called for, among other things, by the new Holy Week rite. Gregorian psalmody is the unmatched genius from which the rest of the body derives, and along with the hymns would have been the easiest element to adapt. There has been no end of Gelineaus since, one more limp than the next, none perennial enough to establish a tradition of congregational song.

There will be no congregational song unless it is braced by

some sort of tradition, something partially static, good or bad. There was enough of a Gregorian ear left to have allowed the frank chant adaptations in the first English missal a chance. They may have been hurriedly done, but they were far better— because they were the work of a competent music advisory board—than the skimpy International Committee on English in the Liturgy (ICEL) offerings in the present book. (ICEL now manages both text and music.) What's left of them has been squeezed into an appendix. They are by now flourishing where they were kept. One can go into St. Peter's Church in downtown Chicago almost any time and hear as heterogeneous a congregation as is likely to be assembled anywhere sound off the original Our Father like a company of marines. In the total context of possible Gregorian adaptation, the missal chants are a small but vital thing, for sooner or later it will become clear that if there is to be a "leader of song," liturgically and psychologically, it had best be the leader of the assembly.

The musically harried priest, however, has not been given much of a chance. If he has been lately ordained and happens to have had new chants drilled into him in the seminary, he will find that they are no longer new, and that there is the promise of more to come. For the oldster the problem is augmented beyond recall: having been mostly acquainted with Gregorian notation (some variation of which might just as well have been preserved), he was, in the very first instance, thrown by the appearance of the vertical lines and crooks attached, wondering whether, according to their disposition, they too indicated scales up and down.

England's latest missal has occasioned the mensuralist battle anew. The introduction of crochets and quavers to undeserving syllables has—I take it on the sufficient word of Dom Gregory Murray—not only stilted oratorical rhythm but murdered the English language. The conscientious cleric must feel a little like the itinerant preacher in Flannery O'Connor's *Wise Blood:* "Where you come from is gone, where you thought you were going to never was there, and where you are is no good unless you can get away from it."

There was, to be sure, no dearth of Gregorian adaptation during the first days of the new creation, but it was not, for the most part, the work of the "scholars and musicians" for whom Father Vitry hoped. Instead it was what he feared: "the fruit of the flimsy essence of amateurs." And it soon vanished. I believe that, given the time and authority, there was enough good will among vernacularists, musicians, and scholars to have established a bridgehead. But about all we could do was tinker at it while the troops went marching by.

Early on, I had Englished a Sunday Vesper Service. It was several years before Vatican II, for I recall employing the fiction that, since it did not follow precisely the specified Roman rite, it would not qualify as a liturgical function but would be allowed as a paraliturgy. What it did follow was the eventually accepted form—three psalms and a longer reading within the traditional framework. It wasn't anything very scientific. Enjoying the necessary textual freedom, musical and literary, we picked and chose through various favorite antiphons that seemed more easily adaptable, pointed psalmody from Douay-Rheims, Ronald Knox, and the Oxford and Augsburg psalter. We inserted a lovely Tallis *Magnificat*—which I had got, I believe, from Ernest White—and, save for an acceptable *Salve,* left the Marian antiphons in Latin polyphonic settings.

Scientific or not, it worked. Weekend's close, at Vesper time, is one of my pleasantest recollections. With the passage of just a couple of years, the Gregorian framework in an English setting was as native to me as ever the Latin was, and some two hundred of us sang it as long as such ventures were possible in our locale. The only people who didn't approve were the people who never came. The idea of the youngsters singing Vespers so galled a coterie of malcontents that one suspected one might genially disembarrass oneself with the supervision of a pot party. But before long most of the boys, as is their wont, were able to essay most of the service, including the psalms, without benefit of books. That, at least, was some kind of scriptural education.

Not that the venture pleased all of my rightist friends. One cold winter evening, Monsignor Johannes Overath[5] and Professor Karl Gustav Fellerer were our guests. I expected them to disapprove of English chant, and they did. Except that Monsignor Overath was kind enough to say that the Tallis *Magnificat* was very nice. But the Tallis was straight Englished Gregorian, adapted, for all I knew, half a dozen times before I finished with it.

One certainly does not quarrel with the strong professional opposition to German chant adaptation, but some of us have questioned the employment of that muscle elsewhere. Thus, at the Fifth International Church Music Congress in Milwaukee in 1966, both English and Latin Vespers were vetoed (the latter for fear of unfavorable reaction from the left) in favor of the Bible Vigil, which even then was on its way out. Years before, I had heard the melodies of the Gradual come through more integrally and beautifully in the Episcopal Church of St. Mary the Virgin than they did in the few New York Roman churches which attempted them in Latin. One might cavil at the tight fit of it all, and I do not know that I should be inclined at present to try much adaptation with the body of the Graduale—any practicality is gone. But the choice between the death of chant and its mutilation need not have been all that stark. Anyway, the history of chant, because of the many elements it absorbed— Hebraic, Greek, Byzantine, Roman, Frankish—is fraught with both literary and musical adaptation, and some mutilation. That is why it is unfair to put all the blame for its misplaced accents on the French and Neo-Solesmes.

I admit to being surprised at the conviction of not a few that the chant will somehow revive. Some envision a phoenixlike recovery. Some cite the rapid sale of used chant editions in a mid-Manhattan music store. (Dessain, Pustet, Schwann, and, until recently, Desclée, have all stopped publishing.) But I think there will be no twentieth-century Romanus the Melodist, or any arch-chanter of St. Peter's, spending two or three years instructing the monks of Northumbria in the music of the Roman chant again.

England and Normandy may well be as desolate as they were in the age of St. Dunstan, but so are Feury and Ghent, from whence came "monks who would take up again the broken tradition, following the same rule, singing the same liturgy, reading the same books and thinking the same thoughts as their predecessors."[6] No, the smallest, hardly thinkable, possible chance has passed, surely never to recur. That was when the

Church might have declared a ten- or twenty-five-year morato-
rium on any kind of music in the liturgy at all. Back to the
catacombs and the harassed church of Ireland—the long silence
damaged neither the faith of the early Christians nor that of the
Irish. The Church might have said, "Look, let us spare ourselves
some years of feckless and futile experiment. Get the best heads
that you can together and prevent what is sure to be a mess.
Take your time, and *think.*"

As it happened, we mostly sat around and fumbled while
Walter Buszin[7] addressed one of our final ecumenical workshop
gatherings: "It is my sincerest hope that your zeal will not
prompt you to seek to solve your problems iconoclastically, as
did some of the reformers of the sixteenth century"; And while
the Fathers at the Council lent but slight ear to the voice of a
more redoubtable churchman: "I am not of the opinion that
because of the Gospel all arts should be rejected violently and
vanish, as is desired by the heterodox, but I desire that all arts,
particularly music, be employed in the service of Him Who has
given and created them . . . and . . . I in nowise desire that the
Latin language be dropped from our service of worship." It was
not the voice of Frings of Cologne or Pizzardo of the Curia. It
was that of Martin Luther of Wittenberg.

WHENCE THE DENOUEMENT?

There are only a few Church musicians around who, like the choirmistress in Galway, hope they don't outlive their pastors. Many of the rest of them are rather in the attitude of St. Paul after being thrown from his horse. They are puzzled, partially blind, and unfortunately not deaf. What they hear are all the dread portents of the Second Coming; and what they see, in the dim-lit vignettes of the Church's music, resembles something less than a picked-over goose. For a year and more I have been asking myself and anyone else whose speech has not been impaired: "How did it all happen? Where did we run aground?"

There was, when the squall was still full-blown, a common response, typical of its violence: "You asked for it." Maybe so. For the Church music fraternity is an odd one, and its undercurrents are sensed by—but mystify—the casual, interested observer. Still, the better part of that fraternity had only followed the dictates of ecclesiastical legislation, and was generally in the vanguard of liturgical propriety and reform. The element of music in the liturgy has ever been considered so vital a factor that a case could be made for liturgical reform having germinated from Church music reform. Witness the phenomenon of Pius X's *motu proprio,* which for a generation appeared to be concerned only with music reform, and so monopolized the appellative that most ordinary folk never dreamed that there had ever been a *motu proprio* about anything else. There appears to be a little more maturity now among the unwashed young, if not in what is left of the genre of the common response. So it might be a safe consideration that the you-asked-for-it response had some occasional subjective value, but was quite short on overall objectivity.

A second response came from those who blamed, with an eye to what billiard players used to call "reverse English," Church music legislation. The writer, not so much assessing blame or cause as offering explanation (dénouement in the sense it was given us in the old English rhetoric classes), will go down, if he goes anywhere, as having belonged to that party. I remember John Finley Williamson saying that you can't legislate taste. (Haydn had said that you couldn't teach it, either.) He was talking about the music legislation of the Roman Church when he said it. He was right, of course, and it was in our laboratory that the great experiment fizzled. I had said at the time that, while a music teacher could not indeed legislate or teach taste, he could do something more important: he could create it. A classic example of begging the question? Perhaps, and perhaps not. Taste, as Paul Henry Lang points out, is a convention, and therefore liable to change.

I think that Williamson's point was that education and climate were, in the long run, more effective arbiters of taste than legislation. If, in his mind or Haydn's, taste were merely some sort of Godkin abstraction, then both teaching and learning are idle pastimes. But if it is indeed a convention, then who is going to affect the next turn of that chameleon but the educator? It can be said for all that legislation that it did attempt, within somewhat straitened terms, to breed a climate of taste; and it did try, without much success, to foster music education. And even if, as the Pauline doctrine runs, law is useless without wisdom and unneeded with it, we should be hard put to blame the vagaries of men on the law instead of on men.

There are two or three variants of this second response. Going from fore to aft, one might consider those who blame not so much the legislation as the lack of it, its loopholes, and its seeds of disintegration. An example of the first instance would be the pastor who called for a wedding blacklist, saying that the only music a prospective bride had requested was stuff from X-rated movies.

A quite prominent European musician and prelate tells me

that the whole business started with the 1953 reform of the Holy Week and Easter liturgies. He borders on the Tridentine, of course, for there could be no overriding criticism of the reform itself. As far as its musical adjuncts were concerned, however, it was promulgated precipitously, and too many were forced to founder for several years in a sea of inept and amateurish Holy Week books—there was no way any of them could be official— that presaged the subsequent frantic efforts of the publishing world to keep up economically with changes that followed one another too fast for absorption. A good deal of that padding is with us still.

It has become customary to say that when any of these ventures comes near to falling flat, it is for lack of pastoral preparation. But a great lot must precede the pastor's work, and no two months of catechesis is likely to overturn the pastoral preparation of centuries.

A further, and it seems to me slightly more thoughtful, notion is that the encyclical, *Musicae Sacrae Disciplina,* and its subsequent 1958 Instruction, represented too much of a shoring up of previously held positions; that these failed to take into account the opposition to current convention that was already obvious then; and that, in attempting to place a finger in the dike, they did in fact open the floodgates of misty interpretative power with a hieratic roulade of the degrees of *participatio.* They are not ignoble documents, but they are only slightly more realistic than Pope John's *Veterum Sapientiae.*[1] The climate was not one of listening to fatherly pleas; it was one of planning to outlive them. A policy of gradualism might have given a better chance to Pope Paul's later cry for the maintenance of an organic link with the past.

A third response is bruited about mostly in the academic community, and it posits the problem as far back as the *motu proprio,* sometimes pursuing it the whole way to Trent. One scholar writes: "I have come to believe that most of the present troubles stem from the *motu proprio* of 1903, which was a bit of deliberate archaism and also wishful thinking. Things have been falling into a kind of musical dichotomy ever since . . . The healthiest times for Church music seem to have been those when it was simply the best of the time—notably, ca. 1480–1530 and the second half of the 18th century."[2]

The archaism leaned in part on the sprouting science of musicology and on the wishful thinking that is ever an earmark of reform, taking an especially romantic turn if it happens to be liturgical reform. Surely the Cecilian goings-on in Regensburg were part of the inspiration of the *motu proprio,* and it is claimed that the document was conceived at a conference in Cologne. Franz Xavier Haberl had invaded the libraries of Trent and the Vatican, and Rome was sending students north for an education in the Church's music. The redoubtable Lorenzo Perosi, for example, was turned down for want of professional training at the Lemmensinstituut in Malines where, under the guidance of Edgar Tinel, the dichotomy between sacred and secular was not overly pronounced.[3] He was accepted at Regensburg, where Franz Witt was having trouble convincing his colleagues that contemporary composition ought to exist side by side with Gregorian and Palestrina.

It is true that until a hundred years ago all Church music was contemporary. The body of the works of most composers was gently put aside, usually forgotten, once their generation had used them. It remained for men like Franz Liszt and Richard Wagner to rhapsodize a chant and a Palestrina they scarcely knew. But it is probably not true that the Roman Church was cut off from the mainstream of music at one fell swoop by the *motu proprio.* For it did, in some ways, epitomize previous pronouncements.

Thus, in its disparagement of the use of instruments in church, it follows the early eighteenth-century rebukes of the Benedictine nuns in Milan and of the Franciscans for using instruments other than the organ. In 1749, an encyclical of Benedict XIV prohibited, among other things, the use of flutes, trombones, and kettledrums. But by 1884, someone had got a foot in the door and these instruments were again permitted "on account of the improved manner in which they are now used as compared to former times."

In 1842 and 1856, Cardinal Petrizi, in the names of Gregory XVI and Pius IX respectively, prohibited the use of instruments in Roman churches, with only a few exceptions; and they were to be used, after proper permission had been secured, only in accompanying the singing.[4] Piux X's mooted exclusion of women from choirs may well go the whole way back to St. Paul's admonition that they keep quiet in church.

Then there is that malicious little old piece of legislation that prohibited nuns from singing the *turba* chants of the Passion under pain of suspension—not specifying withal from what they would be suspended. There was this about the *motu proprio* though: No one would ever again write, as did the Jesuit professor of aesthetics at Valenburg: "Naturally, it would be undesirable to accustom the people to sing rather than pray." Still, the *motu proprio* was a pretty puritan venture. If, as it declared, "modern music has risen mainly to serve profane uses" and was therefore to divest itself of any and all "profanity" before receiving sanction, whose fault was that? And the term "modern" could be forced to cover nearly all known music including Gregorian chant, which, as Paul Henry Lang insists, did not so much grow out of the liturgy as grow into it.

There was also that specific predilection for polyphony "of the Roman school," which could be excused in 1903, but not so readily in succeeding documents that constantly mirrored it. But then Pius bore down most specifically on the Italian theatrical style, and perhaps that is one reason why not all that much attention was paid to his strictures in the classical strongholds north of the Alps, the homeground of Haydn, Mozart, Schubert, and Beethoven, who were roundly excoriated by commentators elsewhere. (A tongue-in-cheek reason, however, for the Italian theatrical style is fully in evidence in many of the Viennese and Bohemian masses.)

Front-line composers, when of a mind to set liturgical texts, didn't pay much attention either, not even the devout Anton Bruckner, whose gigantic effort, had there been any reciprocity between St. Florian's and Ratisbon, might have given events a different turn prior to the *motu proprio.* But where they were applied, they pretty much anesthetized the music of the Church against anything really contemporary. Even in the United States, where not too much beyond Leonard's *Mass in F* was affected, many people felt deprived of a holiday on their holy day.

It was one thing to hold that all Church music must be as

simple and grave as the chant, when chant wasn't always simple and certainly not grave. It was quite another to produce something more than the pale imitative Cecilian onslaught, allowing only occasionally for the tentative chromaticism of a Griesbacher of Filke, or the second-rate Puccini imitations that perdured in the Pontifical Academy at Rome. There were scattered attempts by men like Hendrick Andriessen, and before him Diepenbrock. But it would not be until near mid-century that composers like Flor Peeters and Jean Langlais, Hermann Schroeder, Olivier Messiaen, and Francis Poulenc came up with anything new, whether modal or modern. If, as Louise Cuyler said, the best Church music was usually the best music of its time, it was in large part because it had been enriched by secular experience, and not despite all those factors which the *motu proprio* decried. To say that the present extreme reaction is explained by the *motu proprio* is not to say that it is justified thereby, any more than Versailles justified Hitler or corruption in the Church justified schism. One may or may not assent to Fellerer's compartmentalization of the history of Catholic Church music into music *of* worship (Gregorian chant), music *for* worship (polyphony), and music *at* worship (Baroque and the rest).[5] But we must know that we have more music *at* worship now than ever before.

If all of that great Church music since the age of polyphony must be buried, then logically the churches for which it was written should have been leveled, for the architecture and music of worship are ever twins. The people of Austria and southern Germany, for example, were allowed to keep their rococo churches; and one supposes that is why, despite all the Roman denials of legitimacy, they have kept their music, too. "Worship celebrated in such buildings," said E. I. Watkin, "seems veritably a dance." And the vast Jesuit effort to spiritualize the willful onslaught of humanism was at least as successful as any present pharmacopoeia addressed to the confrontation with secularism, whose tidy concrete bunkers seem only to call for Muzak.

Finally, it is said that the tragic rupture of music and liturgy dates back to the Council of Trent, that its insistence on the Palestrinian ideal was an impossible goal, and that it thereby condemned the previous flowering of the secular *chanson* into the bright glory of Church-oriented composition, and forever discouraged her gathering of her children's multiple talents again. Just how pure the "Palestrinian ideal" was, however, is open to question. It is true that, more than any of his progenitors, he was concerned most exclusively with sacred music, and was the veritable high priest of it. Fellerer credits him with turning from the secular to the sacred *cantus firmus*, but he composed a *L'Homme Armé Mass* as late as 1582, calling it *Missa Quarta*. Other composers at the time of Trent and after—Victoria was an exception—similarly camouflaged their masses with titles like *sine nomine*. And Cerone, in his very influential treatise (1613), begins the chapter on how to compose a Mass with: "Take a good chanson tune!"

So, I take Trent's part in the promulgation of that ideal to be as mythical as the genesis of the *Pope Marcellus Mass*. Trent has, in any case, become a convenient whipping boy for the disaffected; and, ecumenical yearnings aside, anyone concerned about its being straitlaced should take a good look at the classic Chemnitz *Examination of the Council of Trent* for a bilateral view.

It would seem that in the practical realm, the chief and altogether legitimate effect of its strictures was to guard against textual mutilation—something that did not interfere with the baroque cathedrals of sound that were structured upon that integral text almost on the heels of Trent. And although it may seem to have banished a good many parodies,[6] most of these had by then been forgotten, along with their composers, excepting maybe Josquin, whom Luther so admired. It is likely that no one but their composers ever recognized them as parodies anyway.

It is said that the matter of using the *chansons* for the musical basis of a text didn't even come up at the Council. And in the years since the burgeoning investigations of Proske and Haberl, we have been provided with as many settings of the liturgy (parodied or not, *l'homme armé, sine nomine,* it no longer matters to anyone but the musicologist) as could likely have been used all through the intervening centuries. Surely giants like des Prés, Lassus, de Monte, and Byrd were not banished, albeit in Rome they knew mostly Palestrina, Victoria, Anerio, or Suriano; and what there was of the polyphonic tradition would continue, open new vistas in Monteverdi and Fux, and never quite die.

There were those zealots at Trent who wished to do away with all polyphony but, except perhaps in their own bailiwicks, they didn't get very far. The Council ended in a general admonitory tone, asking that anything not in keeping with the dignity of the service be avoided, and leaving any specifics up to the local hierarchy. The sweeping resolutions attributed to Trent's twenty-second session are, in the opinion of Lang, the interpretative resolutions of following generations. The worry went as far back as Augustine and the early Christians' care to insulate themselves from pagan rites.

For myself, I am no longer so sure about the business of legislating taste. Unless we are to be subjected to something worse than universal "kitsch," there must be some built-in safeguards; and maybe "legislation" is not a dirtier word than "guidelines." In a piece called "Second Thoughts,"[7] I suggested in 1966 that, if the Catholic Church Music Association of America had a mission at all, it was "patiently to create, as all teachers must, what St. Paul calls a taste for the things that are above. Diligently to encourage such pockets of taste as dot the flotsam of our legislative wreckage." I guess I began having third thoughts when my own pocket was swept into the vortex, not by pastor or congregation, but by Masters of Social Work.

The sparse generalities of Articles 112–121, Chapter Six of the Constitution on the Sacred Liturgy, have not worked. Inability to legislate taste doesn't mean that you stand by and let bad taste run rampant. The Church, as the architect and custodian of worship, shares in a custodial mission more than anyone. Most bishops vigorously denied that the Liturgical Conference—whose stance was that "the liturgical movement is not 'arty,' it is almost brutally practical in its view of the arts and aesthetic values"—was and would be calling the shots. But it was, and in the end, though it offered nothing so practical as art, it turned out to be brutal enough.

The assumption all along was that everyone, especially the young, was bored with the carefully wrought formality of worship and the artistic design in which it was enshrined.[8] The leaders were perhaps bored. Boredom is a frightful thing. It is the frustration of being subject to inanity. It is the failure of the adult to open for the young a sense of wonder. It is the lost world of underachievement. And that is where we are.

There are indications all over Christendom, from St. Peter's Square to experimental stations in the new catacombs, of extravaganzas winked at. In the United States we have had everything but Bernstein's *Mass* at half time in the Super Bowl. If the Church should decide that, for the record at least, she has the right and the duty to do some negative legislating as an arbiter of taste, her scions would be kept in session well beyond any foreseeable holiday. For centuries, she displayed a genius for transforming pagan festivals into religious celebrations, witness Saturnalia turned Twelfth Night. One might be forgiven one's skepticism over the weight of her thrust in our Bacchanalian times, when the shades of the old Romans must perceive us with admiring awe, as they wonder, perhaps, why, with the media at our disposal, we haven't yet sold Santa Claus a razor. And the suspicion will not down that a good part of the trouble is that there are more boy-bishops than bishops.

BENEFICENT BOMBS

I remember the fuss created by a critic of the institutional Church in the late thirties who called himself Peter Whiffen. What I remember most about him is the respect he had for bartenders. And I suspect that a bartender would have sense enough not to join anything but the Bartenders' Union, and maybe something as highly disorganized but nonetheless organic as his cronies' poker club. For myself, anyone would have thought I might have got all the clubbiness out of me during my school days, when of a spare evening, a companion would taunt me with "What, no meeting tonight?" Still, one is badgered by invitation, by flattery, by the tenuous notion that joining might do someone or something some good. More dire than joining is that moment when, faced with the evidence that one's random memberships are not getting the job done, one imagines that the solution is to start an organization oneself. When it was all over, I wrote about the lack of musical direction following the Council: "From all sides, to all of us, the cry will rise, '*You* do something about it!' Frankly, I can't. I admit only to some small competence which I can exercise in my own corner. Nothing more. It cannot be transferred by workshop or correspondence course. I thought so long ago and have come, more often than not, to regret second thoughts."

So, I have come to think that the splendid old Irish pastor who eschewed any and all parish societies because his parish was society enough was probably right. In the main, organizations leave an imprint mostly where their soul-members would have left an imprint anyway. And on the side they lend respectability to all manner of superficial hangers-on. It is unfortunate but true that organizations, conventions, and workshops attract large numbers who expect to acquire by osmosis what they haven't acquired by study and work. And these are usually the ones who will advertise that they have studied with some celebrity, when actually they have only been resident on the same campus for a short time, attended a lecture or two, and taken a couple of lessons. By the time they have finished making the rounds, they've "studied" with everyone worth mentioning. There is no sense, though, in being a crank about all this. No need to demean the good will, the unselfishness, the lost toil of all us planners. And perhaps now and then there is something to the business of osmosis in the long run. How else does one acquire taste? Who is to say that one gets it, like original sin, a-borning? So what follows is not meant to be as pejorative as it might sound.

Meetings may turn out to be bombs, but there are random acquaintances that turn out to be valuable lifelong associations. Format may be a bore, but there are the smoke-filled rooms of useful exchange, sometimes leased by publishers who are better educators than the Educators. An occasional lecture by a don who, on the chance that no one but his friends will catch on anyway, will say things he wouldn't say in print.

There is a connection between Church music organizations and Church music legislation, of course. It is a little like the business of civic and political groups pretending to do what they say the government isn't getting done. Beside that, though, the Church organization will lean heavily on the wisdom of official documents. Thus the old ACTU (Association of Catholic Trade Unionists) derived from the great labor encyclicals of Leo XIII and Pius XI. (Nobly enough, I thought, though I once heard Bill Green, then president of the A.F. of L., praise them with faint damn as an unnecessary good.) And what with the *motu proprio* and all its progeny, musicians have never wanted for substance and ammunition.

Even if, when you want to start a club, you find no clear mandate for its existence, you do not eschew legislation. You set about laying careful plans for new legislation that will justify your club and banish someone else's. Such a stance is known as the radical left—or the radical right, depending upon how you look at things. Once you get the legislation, you may cease and desist, or move on to something else. Thus *Amen*, a vociferous vernacularist journal, has fallen into oblivion, and the American Liturgical Conference has come upon difficult times, for there are only a few "iffy" items like women's lib to talk about. In my view, both machines should be reactivated: the one to translate the "vernacular" into English; the other to restore the liturgy. The organizations that will come under our purview here, however, are mostly representative of the radical center. Dead center, as a matter of fact. But that is the trouble with the center. If it is indeed a position of balance, you don't want to get off it and no one else wants to get on, at least no one with the juices of the Great Crusade.

A cartoon depicts three or four business executives musing over cocktails, and one of them says, "The trouble with these centrists is that they're too damn far to the left." Draw the converse picture, and you have an idea of the scary existential pose of the centrist. That said, this centrist might be permitted a last nostalgic look at his clubs.

There is the case of the NCMEA (National Catholic Music Educators Association), in my view, an example of two distinct opportunities lost. It was, to begin with, an adjunct of the NCEA (National Catholic Educators Association) which, granted the vast parochial school network, was certainly a validly conceived organization. Had the musical wing, the NCMEA, been geared to securing the integration of music with the total educational scheme, particularly on the secondary level, it might have become a real trailblazer. For then, as now, music outside the very primary grades was considered frosting on the cake and not any kind of academic discipline. A loose social discipline, perhaps, but not one measuring up to the Platonic notion of its use. It was the same in schools generally, and so it is no surprise that so daring an overview was lost, if it was ever thought of.[1]

In any event, the NCMEA soon left the NCEA to strike out on its own. I say "strike out" advisedly, for it missed a second opportunity to trailblaze: the integration of music education with the music of the Church. It never happened, though it was at least talked about. My own minimal participation was always assumed to be concerned with primary-grade music, since I had a boys' choir, and boys were equated with "little" boys. Actually, I was much more intrigued with the proper vocalization of the maturing boy. The former were no problem if you didn't ruin them with a lot of fool adult vocal expertise, and the latter need not have sung, as Sir Richard Terry once observed, "as badly as you let them." In fact, they were almost universally *let.* At one of my first conventions (Philadelphia 1949, I think) the only high-school boys I observed were piano movers.

In the area of music education, NCMEA became a ghetto organization. One would not have objected to that particularly if it had determined to serve its ghetto, the Church. And if it had laid out a whole educational prospectus based on the musically educative values of Gregorian chant—such as reading, singing, and structure, Liturgy or no, the chant does afford just such a universal basis for music education, even after the arrival of Kodály and Orff. I know, because Moe[2] and I have tried it. Instead, the so-called Liturgical Department became a ghetto within a ghetto, and mountains of good will and organizational drive were frittered away in increasingly bland annual meetings.

To have assented to the organization's blurb was to be committed to the proposition that there was somehow a Catholic manner of playing the fiddle or piano. What there was, was only a Catholic manner of blowing one's horn. We had more profitably met with the public education counterpart, the Music Educators National Conference, where there was a broader spectrum of talent, expertise, and money. Some of us did, and we were received with open arms and allowed ample time for parochial considerations. The mere presence of chant and polyphony sessions engendered in those years an interest as in forbidden fruit, and we were its appointed guardians. Twenty years later we would be onlookers!

There was, one fears, no great desire to rub elbows with one's peers. Better a big fish in a pond than a school of minnows in a lake. The attitude has not completely vanished. A competent enough director of a Catholic group recently averred that he never invited professional critics to his concerts. I could say quite a lot about critics, and may, but the ultimate rebuff is *not* to be panned by them. One can possibly learn something from that: it's the consideration that it is not worth their while to show up at all.

Since these paragraphs were written, the NCMEA has bowed out to something called the NPM (National Association for Pastoral Musicians)—whatever a pastoral musician is. A calm one, maybe. Anyway, the NPM has informed the CMAA (Church Music Association of America, about which more shortly) that they want to cooperate but that they cannot share their lists, which probably are comprised of the entire National Catholic Directory. The NPM folder promises "self-starting training sessions," with a discount to members. The first issue of its journal, *The Pastoral Musician,* "will state 'where we are' in music"—and the rest. I suspect that the problem will not be where we are, but that the NPM might take us there.

If one was unhappy with the NCMEA and still felt the need for a club, where could one turn? The American Society of St. Cecilia had been dormant for more than a generation. The Society of St. Gregory, though it still held board meetings and conferred an annual award, was quite as dead. There was Clifford Bennett's recently established Gregorian Institute of America (GIA),—a kind of mammonic certificate and degree mill—but unless you didn't know that Mocquereau and other ghosts, who were advertised as part of the GIA staff, were dead as Marley, you didn't *join* it, you were *taken in.* Frank Campbell-Watson was setting up a Roman Catholic corner in the kingdom of the American Guild of Organists (AGO) with the choirmaster test, but the age of musical ecumenism was far away.[3] One joined the AGO, to be sure, but mostly for reasons of prestige, and to let the kindly local chapter know that we were not all dummies.

I have some notes scribbled variously on hotel stationery (the Arlington in Binghamton, the Stratfield in Bridgeport) which testify to a long-forgotten but high-minded piece of initiative by Fathers Ermin Vitry, Francis Brunner, Richard Schuler,[4] and myself. We would call ourselves the Friends of Sacred Music, and publish a modest service letter through the good offices of Vitry's Fides Jubilans Press. I think one service letter appeared, and I don't believe I contributed.

But when Arthur Reilly, of the McLaughlin and Reilly Publishing Company, generously offered us *Caecilia*,[5] we decided to try to pump some life into the old Cecilian Society. Its aim was "to foster all efforts toward the improvement of Church musicians: choirmasters and choirs, organists, composers and publishers of liturgical music, and through all of these a sound musical approach to congregational participation." We never succeeded in imposing standards upon members by means of examinations in the way the AGO sometimes has. But we had a journal in which we could speak as we pleased. When we were darkly accused of being divisive, warned that salvation lay under one large tent (the NCMEA), we replied that the show might be the biggest there but not necessarily the best. And when someone drearily suggested that we were trying to reestablish the Medicean chant, or when Cliff Bennett (after some verbal asides with his GIA) flew out to Omaha to sue us, "it was," as the old professor said, "to laugh." The society is still incorporated in the State of Nebraska, and though it lasted but nine years, it was around to help establish what many of us saw as the last great hope, the Church Music Association of America.

Sometimes organizers would seize upon just one aspect of ecclesiastical legislation and work it for all it was worth. One such aspect, smaller than some seemed to wish, had been pointed up by Pius X in his *motu proprio:* "Thus, if one wishes to use the high voices of soprani or contralti, these should be performed by boys, according to the most ancient custom of the Church." With no advance warning, I found myself getting mail addressed to the "American Vice President of Pueri Cantores." When Abbé Maillet scoured about the poorer sections of Paris and came up with Les Petits Chanteurs à la Croix de Bois, he may not have envisioned a twentieth-century Children's Crusade but he certainly managed to enlist preachers for it. The then Monsignor Montini gave the Paris-based "General Delegate" credentials to the Apostolic Delegate in the United States, and almost overnight anyone who had been engaged in boy choir work, even if the boys were seminarians, was nominated a "regional delegate." I suppose it was made plain to everyone that there were no duties involved: ". . . honorary . . . no actual work . . . on occasion you can speak about the movement in your travels." Or maybe the General Delegate suspected that, despite my genuine admiration for the work of Abbé Maillet (who was more critical of his own work than some of his critics, like Virgil Thomson), I would be a laggard.

I think that my obeisance to the notion of boy choirs has been sufficient to allow my saying that there is nonetheless an appalling amount of drivel written about them—and a corresponding amount of drivel pounded into the poor kids. Besides this gaseous ethos, the Pueri counted on all the old prejudices of the Church's legislation and, one fears, the horrible example of the Roman choirs. It was still being debated whether Pius X had actually meant "levites" when he said that everything not chanted by the ministers must be sung by the choir of levites. And choir, in the Roman interpretation, signified the architectural arrangement of capitular and monastic churches quite as much as it did any chorus. The ladies of the choir were excoriated by such withering instruments as Carlo Rossini's "Symphony in Black and White,"[6] a privately distributed diatribe against Clifford Bennett, then choirmaster at Sacred Heart Church in Pittsburgh, but directed as well against anyone else who dared to use women in Catholic Church choirs. They were suffered only if, again, "choir" could be architecturally equated to gallery. In a St. Louis church, an exemplar of liturgical propriety, the children of the schola formed a circle, the male half within the sanctuary, the rest without: no hanky-panky in *that* "Ring."[7]

In any case, boys would do. The proper place, the proper garb, and for all that anyone cared, the proper music. Some of us were lucky that the prohibition against heretics in the choir seemed to have been forgotten; the best group I've heard is the Little Singers of Tokyo, whose Christian percentage must be quite small, and which is likely a choir of cordial little heretics, Buddhists, and Shintoists.

The white, ample-sleeved alb and capuche flitted through the lands of West and East like a diminutive Red Cross nurse chasing the 1918 flu. It was all well-intentioned; it did perhaps give boys a musical status; and it occasioned some singing passing fair, as well as a good deal of emoting from Rome to Chicago, where Cardinal Stritch addressed some 2,000 duly invested youngsters as "my little lambs." And it was all quite long ago.

By the time of the International Church Music Congress in Chicago-Milwaukee, the American committee sensibly shied away from its becoming yet another boy choir festival. There is now an American Boy Choir Federation, not especially church-connected. Its last newsletter listed some thirty-two boy choirs whose directors had been, or perhaps would be, replaced. The boys will be next.

It might be added that these organizations have supplied some small repertorial service, but I have found a lack of extensive, personal repertorial diligence to be the besetting sin of too many choirmasters. And the number of folk who assume that there is a sizable body of music written specifically for boys' voices is astonishingly large. That has provided an ineluctable temptation for music education buffs and publishers to exploit with reams of ersatz stuff an animal called the *cambiata*. Castrati, of course, are not presently in vogue, though one wonders when some clod might engineer their return. For, on occasion, for no particular reason that I can think of, one is still expected to suffer the shrill virtuosity of the male alto.

The last great adventure on the American side was the formation of the Catholic Church Music Association of America (CMAA) in August 1965. Or so it hoped to be. It was largely the work of Father John Selner, S.S., and myself, he representing the Society of Saint Gregory, and I that of Saint Cecilia. The idea seemed good enough, and more's the pity that the ideal proved not strong enough to encompass the real. It was meant to be a "saviour," but I keep thinking of the little Luxembourger boy, Jeannot, who came up to me after the Good Friday liturgy, forlorn and shaking his head. "Yo," he said, "Yesus is kaput."

Neither organization amounted to much, but each had supported a journal for a total of nearly 150 years. There wasn't any hatchet to bury then anymore, for the nearest thing to an editorial disagreement that I recall was our objection to what we considered the negativism of their "White List" as over and against what they were pleased to call our "Golden List." The journals, with their meager assets, would coalesce, and the societies would submerge themselves into one with a constitution

broad enough to serve as an umbrella for most concerned practitioners. The idea was to place itself at the service of such
segments of the American hierarchy as would be concerned
with carrying out the instructions of Vatican II.

That the seams of this patchwork tent eventually gave way to
internal bickering and were finally rent wide open, this time by
the rightist sector, is now beside the point. The possibility was
there. Cardinal Dearden gave the idea his personal approval
and asked each of us to submit a list of competent professional
musicians who could be counted on to serve as a national music
advisory board.

There was no political machination about this, though it was
being bruited about that one or the other individual, not especially interested in a joint effort, was sitting on the Cardinal's
doorstep in Detroit. It was a legitimate offer of service and one
appreciated by the Cardinal. To this day, Father Selner and I
have no idea who was on each other's list, except that we had
mutually agreed not to list each other. But I suspect that between us we placed a majority of the membership of the original
bishops' music advisory board. It comprised a formidable array
of knowledgeable personnel. At the time, the impression was
abroad that all or most of the vernacular offerings would somehow have to be approved, and diocesan music commissions
were proceeding accordingly. As it turned out, the only things
at stake were such items as would appear in the official Mass
books: Prefaces, responses, and the like. There would be no
counterpart of the official Latin service books that had been
revised and issued from 1905 onward.

After meeting a few times, the board was expanded, key people were replaced or resigned, and it lost all semblance of a
broadly based team of musicians and scholars working toward
ultimate and well-defined goals. It is now, as far as anyone is
concerned, as defunct as its British counterpart. (ICEL, the
International Committee on English in the Liturgy is now in
charge.) But let it be said that its work for the early provisional
books outclassed what followed.

Perhaps the notion of a single, all-embracing organization
like the CMAA was not viable to begin with. Certainly the temper of the times was against it. There were those liturgists who

viewed any gathering of musicians not molded according to their specifications with suspicion and some alarm. There was an implied and insensate condemnation of Church musicians, for example, in Norbert Höslinger's commentary on the constitution.[8] He held that Article 113 "decides the fate of Church concerts with a liturgical accompaniment at the high altar." And there were musicians, to be sure, who viewed any cooperation with the Liturgical Conference as something akin to sin. While I had not shared the hope, long or recently nurtured by some of our collaborators, that the Liturgical Conference was going begging for really professional help, I was dismayed and angry when members of the CMAA board resorted to parliamentary artifice to block our sponsorship with them of the Kansas City Forum which produced "A Crisis in Church Music."[9] What was said in that brochure would have been said anyway, and without any reflections of our points of view.

The Association managed to host the first meeting of the International Consociatio (CIMS) at Chicago-Milwaukee, and the polarization evident there was complete by the time of its Boston convention two years later. An appeal to the bishops for support had brought little response and one or another scolding. The far right retrenched. Most others, like the Sugar Creek–Missouri composers' group[10] left, and the CMAA stance became indistinguishable from Una Voce.[11] That organization, whatever it says now, was traditionalist in the Tridentine sense, hardly now *una voce*. So the CMAA is now as dead as its predecessors. About this the present board feels no particular grief, and certainly no compunction. It still manages to publish its journal, *Sacred Music,* venerable now in Volume 103, and one hopes that its recent disclaimer of extremist positions can be believed. Not having much else to do at the moment, I think of rejoining.

Consociatio Internationalis Musicae Sacrae (CIMS)

On November 22, 1963, the sixtieth anniversary of the *motu proprio,* Pope Paul, in a chirograph, established the "International Consociatio for Sacred Music" (CIMS). On December 4, the conciliar Fathers, together with the Pope, would promulgate the Constitution on the Sacred Liturgy. The latter was published in January of 1964, the former a few weeks later. Monsignor Romita,[12] in his commentary in the *Desclée Monitor Ecclesiasticus,* saw a sequential link: a rearguard maneuver of a small group of devoted Church musicians on the one hand; the bishops of the world, unwarrantedly basking in the full glory of the official fruition of years of liturgical endeavor, on the other; and the Pope on both sides.

There were, it was said, the essential seeds of such a society in the ancient institutions of the Roman Schola Cantorum, the Cappella Pontificia, the late sixteenth-century Congregation of St. Cecilia (radix of the State Academy of St. Cecilia), and in the nineteenth-century proliferation of Cecilian and Gregorian societies. More proximately, there was the Association of the Friends of the Pontifical Institute of Sacred Music. At the First International Congress of Sacred Music in Rome in 1950, the vice-president of the Friends, the redoubtable Josquin scholar, Albert Smijers, had suggested just such a thing as the Consociatio. And at the Fourth Congress in Cologne in 1961, Cardinal Frings had agreed to bring a preliminary schema to the attention of the Holy See. Its purpose would be to carry out the acts of the Congress, with the much-needed pontifical muscle. Existing societies and independent scholars would be invited to affiliate. There would be the usual elected officers, the president and secretary requiring confirmation by the Holy See, the secretary a resident in Rome. The delegates to future Congresses ought to be official representatives of their respective bishops. Reporting to whoever read *Caecilia* that fall, I wrote that it was my guess that it was not the Holy See but the Allgemeiner Cäcilien Verband (ACV), the Cecilian society for German-speaking peoples, that was "behind the move toward a universal Roman axis. While one admires this spirit of submission, one hopes that it might not lead to a too monolithic musical hegemony."

I guess I had been a little nonplussed by the spectacle of the older Regensburg establishment seeking affiliation with the Pontifical Academy, when I thought it high time that the Pontifical Academy affiliate with someone itself. I don't think it was any specter of *Realpolitik,* for I had not forgotten my first trip through the Brenner Pass. Goethe's Hoch Altare kept looming up at sudden, random curves as we headed for its narrow and beautiful wiles. Up there, where one must crouch to the bottom of the train window to see, were trees and rocks and sunlight. And at Brenner the still pure twilight and the evening star seem to shrive the place of the machinations of Hitler and Mussolini.

The Cologne proposition pretty much spelled out the sum and substance of *Nobile Subsidium Liturgiae,* Pope Paul's chirograph. The status of the Consociatio was that of a moral person, under the patronage of the Prefect of the Congregation of Rites. Its purpose, that of a resource person to help the apostolic see solve the problems proper to its field, "effective because it would be in constant touch with the supreme authority of the Church." (But the supreme authority would also have to be effective.) It would "promote cooperation and harmonious action among the societies existing throughout the world."

The monolithic hegemony was there too: members *de jure* would be the Institutes of Sacred Music approved by the Holy See and their affiliates. That meant, I take it, the Roman Pontifical Institute, probably the Ambrosian Pontifical Institute of Sacred Music in Milan, and the following: the School of Pius X at Manhattanville (now defunct), St. Michael's Choir School in Toronto, the School of Music of DePaul University in Chicago, the Church Music School of Regensburg, the Escuela Superior of Guadalajara, the Higher Institute of Sacred Music of the University of St. Elizabeth of Hiroshima, and the Escuela Superior of Mexico City. Although inbred, a decent but hardly a world-shaking aggregation.

Pueri Cantores headed the list of "properly recognized" societies of Sacred Music. Members *de jure* and "the delegate of each nation, selected by the bishops," were to have a deliberative vote, all other voices being consultative and passive. The national commissions of Sacred Liturgy and Music of which the Constitution spoke (Articles 44–46) were not to be part of the Consociatio. It was to serve them—and try to save itself from them.

The Holy See hadn't had to finance anything so vast as the liturgical lobby, so the patrimony of the Consociatio would consist of dues from the members (there were two kinds, corporate and individual), the gifts of pious benefactors, and returns from the works of the Consociatio. By the fall of 1967, less than 50 percent of its members had paid their dues, and there was the sum of $2,400 in this tremendous international kitty. In the United States alone, the Liturgical Conference was making hay out of prerogative by inference. It had gathered 400 members of diocesan commissions at Kansas City at $50 per registration, and it charged publishers, in line for bread, $150 each in Washington, D.C.

The Consociatio had its biggest American day when it convened the Fifth International Congress of Sacred Music at Chicago-Milwaukee in the summer of 1966. In some ways, it was not unlike the Democratic Convention that would follow in Chicago in 1968. To begin with, there is not much question that the establishment of the CIMS had been eyed with suspicion by the vanguard of liturgical reform. Something more than a straw in the wind was the declaration by the prestigious Austrian liturgical scholar, Josef Jungmann, S.J., to the effect that the fiercest opposition to the liturgical renewal came from the forces of sacred music. In Europe, a kind of counterorganization had sprung up which called itself Universa Laus, the moving spirit of which appeared to be the then popular Père Gelineau.

It's funny how one must be either *una* or *universa,* when each wants really to be both. In this country, the temper of the symposium on sacred music at Kansas City is betrayed in an account by George Devine[13] of a paper prepared by this writer. It was felt by most, he said, that I presumed that "the congregation really isn't capable of participating very much in a sung liturgy." That's not what I said; but Devine, in his reappraisal, was good enough to admit that I had a point. While I had been asked to present the "rightist" position, I felt that I was very much in the middle and insisted on punctuating the given title, "Leaning Right," with a question mark, never having been to the right of anything in my life. What I tried to do, with the energy of Ted Marier, who read the paper, was oppose the mediocrity and cheapness which seemed to me to come close to becoming a liturgical ideal.

Also, in this country, Father Clement McNaspy was delivering dark shafts from his column in *America* at the restrictive goings-on in the CIMS study week in Chicago. I do not think, of course, as some merry-andrew has suggested, that there was some sort of Jesuit conspiracy, dating back to the Society's early and repealed statute of musical bias. But the whole thing was terribly unfortunate, for both the critics and idolators of the Congress were most of them actually its friends, a good many of them loyal voting members of the CMAA. There was not much sense in making conscientious objectors look like traitors on the one hand, or Monsignor Overath like a preview of Richard Daley on the other.

A clear, well-publicized distinction might have been helpful. The study days in Chicago were a meeting of the CIMS; the exemplification days in Milwaukee were primarily a concern of the CMAA. It is a fair presumption that most of the kids in Grant Park were Democrats. To get into the Chicago affair at Rosary College you had to be a dues-paying member, and there weren't many. There were nuns who had to wheedle the fee, a relatively small one, out of their mother superior or a friend, and village organists who paid for it out of their meager stipend.

It is understandable that the number of specially invited guests had to be held to a minimum, though I was also understandably irked when the genial, generous, and scholarly Gene Selhorst, of the Eastman School of Music, had to sit out the affair in the La Salle Hotel, and the American committee seemingly could do nothing about it. Maybe they should have accepted payment of legitimate memberships at the gate, but poor Father Lopez-Calo, S.J., the General Secretary (there goes the Jesuit conspiracy), would probably have been accused of botching up the accounts.

Within the meeting itself discussion was minimal. I remember being put down with no authority at all on the question of electronic music. I wasn't lobbying for it but thought we had better face it, music or not. There were unfortunate and unnecessary denunciations of Universa Laus, a seeming attempt to write off its right to existence. Some of us were members of both groups—had, in fact, tried to steer the CMAA into affiliation with both. But with few exceptions, neither side would counte-

nance a split allegiance. The Consociatio insisted on Universa
Laus affiliating with it, and Universa Laus would have nothing
to do with the people in control of the Consociatio—a pity, for
whatever one thought of the musical spin-offs of Père Gelineau,
they were superior to the trivia of successive inundations. Jean
Langlais, a severe critic, has come to wish they were back in
vogue in France.

Not all of the Universa Laus people were out to play ducks
and drakes with the *thesaurus musicae sacrae,* which even the CIMS
tended to circumscribe. (When Cardinal Suenens once related
to Father Josef Joris, a CIMS delegate and an officer in Universa
Laus, that he thought he had really experienced the Holy Spirit
at a Pentecostal meeting, Josef replied, "Yes, so do I—whenever
I hear Gregorian Chant or Bach.") Both were vitally interested
in new music; Universa Laus in what they considered new and
ancient forms; CIMS, in a scientific structuring of the Church's
music in mission lands. The effort required anything but divisive tactic and personality play. For the music community was
besieged by a demanding army of liturgical pundits who didn't
know what they were demanding, and sometimes cared less.

A degree of harmony would have taken the sting out of ill-
considered barbs like that of Father Jungmann. And the CIMS
might have better fended the frequent charges of *Romanita*
hurled by those who seemed chiefly to want to put Rome in a
corner. The unseemly garrulousness of both sides of the American sector on the last day of the study week and on following
days in Milwaukee caused a not negligible number of well-
placed persons from the academic community, both able and
willing to help, to put Chicago and Milwaukee behind them in
sorrow and disgust. The proceedings of the Congress are published in a book entitled *Sacred Music and Liturgical Reform.*[14] It
contains, besides many meaty chapters, not all of them hewing
to a preordained line, a list of those who crashed the study days
without a wedding garment. The trouble is that those who
should will probably never read the trenchant papers, say, of
Bishop Graber and Eric Werner.

One of the things left unsettled by the rumpus in Chicago-
Milwaukee was the matter of the election of officers. That was
the ostensible reason for calling a "restricted" meeting in Rome

in the fall of 1967. It was a kind of encore to the embattlements of Chicago, only this time the disarray was caused not by ugly Americans but by Europeans.

Some seventy-five people gathered in the *aula* of the Pontifical Institute, most of them for their own edification. For there were listed only fifteen *jure proprio* members with the right to vote, and eleven "aggregate" members, with the right to be aggregate members. The *jure proprio* people were mostly representatives of old-line Church music organizations (The National Catholic Music Educators Association was, by now, somehow affiliated) and Institutes affiliated to the Pontifical Academy. Only one religious order had bothered to organize itself—the Capuchins under Father Peter Peacock, then warden of Greyfriars, Oxford. And only one delegate represented a national conference of bishops, Canon Josef Joris, director of the Lemmensinstituut in Malines, Belgium.

The eleven aggregate delegates were an aggregation indeed: representatives of the Abbey of Solesmes, the Catholic University of America, the Mocquereau Foundation, the German Franciscans, the Wiener Union for Africa—and Father Flanagan's Boys' Home, which was pretty close to Africa.[15]

Very shortly, the position of Canon Joris became a bone of contention. A *nota bene* attached to the list of *jure proprio* members explained that, though the CIMS statutes provided for voting representatives of bishops' conferences, that was only for general assemblies, and since general assemblies could only be held every three years, this was not a general assembly. In the spirit of the statutes, however, Canon Joris was nonetheless allowed to exercise a deliberative vote.

The reunion was all but blown up by its own petard, for it appeared that there were other episcopal representatives present who hadn't been reckoned with. They were eventually allowed to vote too, but not before the basic flaw of a political animal, which wished now to charge authoritatively, now to canter democratically, had demonstrably surfaced. There were no smoke-filled rooms, but I remember being looked upon darkly when I was observed at a sidewalk luncheon with the dissidents, where, indeed, I was smoking furiously. I was sympathetic enough, but not very understanding.

Having gotten the votes, the dissidents were determined to exercise a customary European parliamentary maneuver: protest by not voting. I don't know whether such a move would have sent their bishops scurrying to Rome to investigate the CIMS or not, but to a sometime A.F. of L. rabble-rouser like myself, it made no sense at all. They had a better right than they knew to ill sort out my math, but it was apparent to me that they had enough votes to substantially affect the outcome of whatever they were not going to vote for.

In the end, Dr. Jean-Pierre Schmit was elected president to succeed the ailing Monsignor Overath. It was, he said, a moment of high emotion for him, as he addressed his thanks to the assembly in German, French, Italian, and English. But also, according to the statutes, the president had to be confirmed by the Holy See. And poor Jean-Pierre was never confirmed, though heaven knows he could be accused of being leftish about nothing except his underground activity during the Nazi occupation of Luxembourg. Maybe the assembly was, after all, not an assembly. Or maybe some bishop did scurry.

Few other achievements were alloted to the 1967 venture, unless one counts the standing ovation for Justine Ward, and the financial report of the harried secretary, Father Lopez-Callo, who was more perspicacious than most. In an address before any of the politicking began, he deplored the financial status of the organization, which had remained afloat only because of the largesse of Pope Paul and Monsignor Overath, and a loan from Monsignor Anglès.

He noted that one of the more serious consequences, one that had damaged the reputation of the CIMS, had been his inability to contact the bishops of the world about the statute concerning their conference's delegates to general meetings. He further remarked that the inevitable result of the organization's overcentralization not only paralyzed it, but in the long run would lead to the suicide of the whole initiative. Callo was eventually sacked amid dark muttering about his having loaned the office typewriter to a group of nuns, or some such thing. He is now back to lecturing on musicology—happily, one hopes—in Northern Spain.

Anglès, too, had his eyes open. He called for unity and dialogue, even with "those who think differently from ourselves and may even be in ways different from those of the Consociatio." In the matter of the *thesaurus musicae sacrae,* he asked for a small enough favor: "the preservation, as far as possible, of the Latin ceremonial liturgy, especially in the sung Mass, which should be in Latin at least once on every Sunday and Church holiday."[16]

Anglès further admitted to the existence of extremists "on both sides," but ventured the hope that the "truth and spiritual and pastoral effectiveness of sacred music, in its highest form as art, would again come into its own, even as its secular counterpart is a part of civic education in socialist countries." He called for the creation of a spirit of trust in the Consociatio. He was, indeed, as he said, an optimist.

Perhaps no international organization is equal to the task of dealing with what, given the vernacular, is ultimately a national problem.[17] For all of its efforts in the direction of worthy vernacular settings, the Consociatio drums along in the image of one merely trying to preserve the *thesaurus;* and Universa Laus comes to fairly futile cross-purposes in beholding what different language groups are able to pull off in the way of experimental media. Neither group has any money. At last report, Universa Laus was veering out of the Gelineau orbit into sociological sorceries which musicians frankly did not understand. And the Consociatio was honing down its membership to a select group of scholars. But if you happen to have joined in the bright days of promise, you will not be expelled. You may sit around and listen to the ticking of the beneficent bomb.

AFTER-DINNER LEGISLATION

On January 25, 1964, Pope Paul VI established the *Consilium ad exsequendam Constitutionem de Sacra Liturgia.* Out of it were to come all of those reforms in book, calendar, and ceremonial called for, but not spelled out, by the Council Fathers. While touching sacred music only peripherally, it would gestate the later (1967) "Instruction on Sacred Music."

For a long time, I confess, I was hopeful that a statement from this postconciliar commission, delineating Chapter Six of the Constitution, might clear the air. But the several drafts reflected clearly which group had got its hands on it last, and which would accept it once it saw the light of day. The document is not much quoted any more, but, as might have been expected from the manner of its forming, it carried the seeds of ambivalence,[1] allowing disputants to armor themselves with it, either to protect their own integrity or to badger that of their opponents.

There was, in the published but "secret" elenchus, or listing of consultants to the commission, a fairly generous sprinkling of people known principally as Church musicians, although heaven knows how they were chosen. Completely unforewarned, I learned that I was included at the behest of the Secretariat for Non-Christians. The "relator" for matters musical was Monsignor John Beillard, president of the French Federal Union for Sacred Music. But I do not gainsay for a moment Monsignor Overath's contention that among the actual members[2] of the Consilium there was not a single prelate of musical competence, though several had been known for their forthright speech during the Council. Neither Monsignor Anglès, as president of the Pontifical Institute of Sacred Music, nor the president of the papal CIMS were numbered among the working committees that were entrusted with the various musical problems before the Consilium.

Nor were they invited to attend the meeting of what Annibale Bugnini[3] called "a small group of liturgists and musicians" who prepared the final redaction of the "Instruction on Sacred Music." It appeared that the musical right arms of the Holy See were paper tigers, patterned out of ancient parchments that the strategists found tired. When they did get a point across, they had only the status of those lesser congressional lobbyists who might take credit for a vote, but who are known lightly by the club as "rainmakers." Not soon would Annibale, beyond the Alps, before the gates, be forgotten—or forgiven.

Anyway, as a consultant, I dutifully delivered what were called *animadversiones* to scenarios dreamed up by Bugnini or whomever. They probably read like Frank O'Connor's bibulous father's reconstruction of the *Adeste Fideles: "Solus domus dagus, Dixie medearo, Tuto tonum tantum"* etc. There were three separate skirmishes before the final redaction. In the first draft, the matter of vernacular chant adaptations was aired. One heard nothing of it in subsequent drafts. A curious business. The reformers hadn't the courage to demean the chant outright, in face of Chapter Six of the Constitution.[4] And maybe they knew that speaking of chant adaptation was perfectly safe because the more prestigious of the chant's defenders would not hear of adaptation.

But it seemed to me to be a crack in the door, so I marshalled all my old arguments: it must be an official adaptation, the fruit of the best scholarship available; it must remain the patrimony of the Holy See, else the vaunted restoration of Pius X was in vain. But, I averred, *"sicut dicitur in lingua nostra,* the cow is already out of the barn." Innumerable monkey adaptations, including some of my own, had already been approved by local ordinaries. Though these were sometimes admitted only conditionally and faced the possibility of revocation in the event of a general realignment, they still gather semi-official dust.

It also appeared to me that the draft was really eyeing only a kind of minimal vernacular *Jubilate Deo,* for it declared out of hand that melismatic structures especially lent themselves sparsely to adaptation. Having long since wearied of liturgical pundits on the American scene who lectured us about the inadvisiability of vernacularizing lengthy melismatic chants, since that would be grand opera,[5] I asked the commission what difference it made whether the carrying vowels were sung in Latin, Spanish, French, or English. I steered clear of the diphthongs which make it impossible for most people to sing German and for most Germans to sing anything else. The *jubilus,* quoth I—or was it St. Augustine?—was necessary to the human spirit from pre-Gregorian to the dialectic of American Jazz; and, as long as we happened to be talking about Church *music,* one might note that here the melody was more important than the text.

There was an occasional curious, almost curial, tone to the initial draft that set one to wondering whether Rome was getting ready to turn out the Canadian Rotarians all over again.[6] It was asked, for example, whether concerts of "religious music might be held in the church for a 'most grave' cause." And there was considerable discussion about the propriety of using Latin and the vernacular in the same service. I did not find the *casus* to be *perridiculus.* Some of the American bishops were banning an English *Missa Cantata,* most were banning the Latin, and my own ordinary fretted some because he wasn't sure that he had the authority to allow me the polka dot.

So I responded that the *permixtio linguarum hinc sapienter proposita* was a *sine qua non* for both active participation and the preservation of our musical heritage. That it ought to be obvious that the further the vernacular penetrated, the more the Latin texts would be generally understood. That our heritage would be enriched if we kept at least some parts of the Ordinary in a traditional language, no matter who sang it: the Kyrie in Greek, like the Lutherans and Anglicans, as a *relatio* to the oriental Church; the Agnus in Latin to give the prayer and sign of peace a tinge of universality. Perhaps not a glorious *sequitur,* but then neither was Father Overath's intervention on the

Agnus. Tongue in cheek, he had written that the Agnus need not be preempted for the congregation, as everyone was saying, since the first Agnus had been enunciated by John the Baptist, and on *hearing* it, the Israelites followed Christ. That suggested not a choral, but a cantor role.

A paragraph that gave some small space to the choir seemed well-enough put, but I wondered why no one ever seemed to suggest that particular parts of the *Missa in Cantu* especially became the choir—not just for all the talk about preserving the *thesaurus,* but "on account of the distribution of the ministries, for the glory of God, and the building up of the faithful—and for the good of Christian artists, *qui etiam pars populi Dei sunt.* "[7]

I applauded the relaxed section on the use of instruments in church, noting that well-designed pipe organs and competent organists would be even more necessary for congregational singing, not realizing then that the real issue would be the equivalent of chopsticks-playing guitarists. Finally, I opined that this was certainly the primordial issue: sacred music could not be *pars integrans* of anything unless it was a *pars integrans* of education. Firming up a notion as wild as that—when the astral body of liturgists blithely assumed that music must just happen, like trance-writing—was as futile as the undertakers' lobby fighting Medicare.

The second draft was a wordy affair, spelling out minutiae in the manner of the directions for putting together an artificial Christmas tree, prescribing at least once in every second paragraph safeguards for *participatio actuosa.* It cautioned that when the organ, or indeed a whole battery of instruments, was used, it must be possible to understand the text. It was not clear who was to understand it, since the presumption was that everyone would be singing it. Maybe the Lord was expected to listen— a primitive god would surely have joined the racket and up-staged the participators.

It said something about the possibility of choirs being pre-served in cathedrals and major sanctuaries. Eric Werner had described this as the "Anglican solution," and, with others, urged its adoption. I thought it a little upper-middle-class, and responded that never and nowhere had the choir been so cir-cumscribed, that if they wanted to keep on talking about the choir having a ministry, they should stop hedging.

There was also an elaborate delineation of the manner of confecting the Introit, which reminded one of the old query as to the legality of starting it before the priest left the sanctuary. (A more practical concern would have been how long you might wind up singing!) I suggested that the Asperges—relegated, as it turned out, only into limbo—be incorporated in the Sunday entrance rite. And there was a coals-to-Newcastle emphasis on the hymn option, with a wholesale swipe at the music of the eighteenth and nineteenth centuries which I found "dangerous, negative, and hardly necessary."

In general, I considered the whole to be a summation, not altogether an honest one, of previous documents, and unnecessary for anyone who could read. It was contrary to the spirit of Chapter Six, as a matter of fact, and a *defloratio* of the *motu proprio* of Pius X. I questioned the presumption that liturgical commissions were competent to pass on the suitability of music, and the omission of any mention of the Consociatio or the inferences that might be drawn from its charter. Because it was perfectly plain which scriveners had swiftly scrivened the second gazetteer, I thought it better not to publish an instruction at all.

The third draft mostly avoided the drivel of the second, and would have itself constituted a better document than the final Instruction. Principle was urbanely set forth, and the paths it suggested were middle and sane. About my only objection was to the use of the term "office of commentator." Inimical as that character was to liturgical action, one had hoped that the vernacular Mass would finally have rendered him or her obsolete.

For the rest, the early copies of *Notititiae*,[8] mimeographed then for the edification of the commission's consultants, reveal more dressed bones than the Capuchin cemetery off the Via Veneto. Witness the query as to whether the celebrant must sing the Sanctus even if it happened to be polyphonic (a not altogether unlikely clerical ploy), and this small smattering of dubia which were resolved, it was said, with "orientative" validity:

No, the Consilium never would permit the canon to be said in the vernacular.

The conference of bishops *must* approve the melodies for

vernacular texts of celebrants and ministers, and also of people and schola if these were part of a dialogue or acclamation; and it was up to the individual bishops to check out the propriety of all Ordinary and Proper parts of the Mass.

No, a concession had not been granted to say the Per ipsum in the vernacular, nor was there any hope it ever would be. Not even Bugnini's usual "have patience" here. Little enough patience was needed. Too commonly, in any language, it's not even the minister's anymore. The great Amen is not a response but a dud.

No, that suitable minister who exercised the office of commentator could not be garbed in civilian dress.

Yes, all vernacular missals must contain a marginal Latin text. (If you don't take to the tongue of the locale, you're sometimes lucky if you can find a Tridentine missal in order to say Mass at all.)

No, a religious does not discharge his breviary obligation by saying it *in choro* in the vernacular with lay brethren.

Evil-sounding words like *heretics* and *schismatics* were to be dropped from public prayer, on the presumption, one supposes, that either there were no more, or they needed no public prayer. But if the Consilium and the SRC were fumbling the ball, so were others. In one and the same meeting, the American bishops defeated an amendment that would have put the Prayers at the Foot of the Altar in English, and vetoed another— proposed with legitimate concern by McIntyre and Mueller— that would have added *piam* to *plenam consciam et actuosam participationem.*

Thus, if one should perchance reread the ensuing Instruction, the several that followed, or their manifold "clarifications," and wonder about a certain amount of gobbledygook, he ought not be surprised.

THE EXPERTS

One blustery November afternoon, in the neighborhood of Garmisch, an army chaplain friend of mine got his hands on a cache of canned goods, and we set out to visit one of the several occupation-era Boys Towns that burgeoned in the wake of Father Flanagan's youth missions for the United States government. Although I assured the superintendent that it was not my picture that graced his wall, he insisted on assembling the boys to sing a song for us. As they sang, I noticed the chaplain curl his lip as if he had a cut of Beech-Nut under there, for the boys were giving out, with whatever words, the *Horst Wessel* song. And I hoped, for the sake of those kids, that it was not functional music.

No one since Plato had thought of music as functional, indeed as something moral and necessary as had Hitler, the ultimate Wagnerian, except for a particular breed, new- or half-, of liturgist. The Menninger people lectured briefly about its therapeutic value at music educators' conventions, and there were a couple of concert broadcasts from asylums to prove a point; a not so neat evasion of the possibility that it might have been music which drove the performer mad in the first place. And I remember giving a concert for a group of shell-shocked veterans, being told by the experts not to bother being selective about music that might stir emotions, and to be sure to include, of all things, "Ole Man River." The orderlies had a busy twenty minutes quieting our audience. In the yard, on that day, Helen Wills Moody demonstrated tennis skills to the men, and her performance had all the peaceful air of *Eine Kleine Nachtmusik.*

It is, of course, one of the popular glories of music to be functional—and of painting and architecture. But it remained for quite recent experts to pronounce Lassus and Michelangelo and Chartres unfunctional. They may call the medieval man illiterate, but he read far more Scripture and hagiography in glass and in stone than his twentieth-century counterpart ever will in cartoon and tube, which are fast on their way to erasing all trace of literature.

Ordinary people found art functional enough. The difference was that both patrons and builders understood that to be functional it had to be art. They would not have comprehended the weird analysis of today's experts: "Function has no necessary connection with art, and is indeed better off without it." Untrammeled by gimmicks, they recognized that art was simply skill; that the more skillful a thing was, the more human it became. They needed no academic dissertation on the humanities.

The trouble now is that in music, of all the arts, someone besides the artist is always telling us what it is, what it ought to do or sound like. Professional educators and social workers have decreed that the pupil educate the teacher; the child, the houseparent; and you don't argue with them unless you have been initiated into the abracadabra of their thirty-second degree. Similarly, no mere musician disputes the professional liturgist's revelations about, and arbitraments on, Church music. The numerous commentaries that ensued upon the Instruction of the post-conciliar commission were mostly done by liturgical experts who soon persuaded even bona fide Church musicians that since the liturgy had changed, music, by definition, must change. The nature and function of neither had changed, of course. But it is always safe for a writer not to know what he is talking about if he can presume that his readers won't know what he is talking about.

Whatever the value of the primary documents, some breadth of opinion had usually gone into them. Experts abhor unchained Bibles, however, and the new music instruction, channeled abroad from the Bishops' Secretariat on the Liturgy through the United States Catholic Conference, included a "Clarification and Exhortation," which intimated that the original might not be altogether safe reading. We were told that there were words of comfort for the professional musicians who "falsely" thought that the new liturgy had abandoned the special role of the choir. Too many of them had already been driven to Southern Comfort, and most dioceses could count their choirs on the fingers of a single mangled hand.

Anyway, it was not so much the choir that had been abandoned, but music. It was said that the artificial line between the sung and spoken liturgy was now extinct. What this meant was that we had been shoved back into the worst tradition of the *Sing-Messe.* [1]

A setting of the Sanctus, so the clarification ran, might reflect the highest artistic quality but be an intolerable interruption of the tone and sense of the Eucharistic Canon. Most people were willing to accept that on the evidence of a simple chant like that of *Mass XVIII,* obviously a direct response to the ferial Preface. But there was also the legitimate Anglican contention that of all Mass music, the Sanctus called for the most elaborate artistic endeavor—musical works, the kind of which the Instruction had said that if they no longer had a place in the liturgy but could "nonetheless foster a religious spirit and encourage meditation on the sacred mystery," they might be transferred to popular devotions or Bible services. There were those who felt that such now-fugitive curiosities were more properly places for a musical junkyard, if one had to exist; and that any music "fostering a religious spirit and encouraging meditation" ought bloody well find a place in the liturgy.

A subsequent instruction on the American side would fret about the lack of proportion between the music of the Gloria [2] and the rest of the service of the Word, when what most of God's people worry about is the proportion of the homily vis-à-vis *all* of the rest.

We were to be especially cautious about the Instruction's making provision for "one or more Masses in Latin, especially sung Masses," because some might take it as license "to preserve and recreate the bad tradition of nonparticipating congregations." All those mute, spectating forebears of ours! Dumbness had long since acquired the connotation of stupidity. It is only latterly that *Notitiae* braves a *Tibi silentium laus* and discourses on a "style" of calm. There was the usual lecture about the usefulness of the cantor, and an intimation that he could replace the choir. No cantor in the traditional sense was envisioned, but the "leader of song," the singing commentator who, with voluminous gear at hand, cowed more folk into silence than singing.

The "old distinction of Ordinary parts for the people, Proper parts for the choir" had been eliminated. It was not clear where such a distinction had ever been made, but its elimination was said to be "new to papal documents." Surely few choirs considered the Propers their private preserve, and most were notorious for ignoring them. Finally, we were told that on principle the liturgy should reflect and welcome contemporary music. (Read "hootenanny" for "contemporary" and you could, like Godfrey Diekmann, bring an NCMEA convention cheering to its feet.) But that principle "had been ignored for decades until the challenge of the new vernacular texts arose." There was— I beg your sufferance of a repetition—a good deal more truly contemporary music in our churches in the several decades preceding Vatican II than since. What turned off too many of its composers was precisely the tawdry "challenge" of the new vernacular texts. The experts, apparently, had mostly been honoring the distinction that provided for low Mass.

There was, it is true, Rembert Weakland's blanket assertion that the traditional Church musician had an innate fear of anything new and contemporary, but Iginio Anglès had placed matters in a more proper perspective. Speaking on "Church Music: An Ecumenical View," he had told a congress in Berne that "the contemporary Church composer finds himself in a dilemma: If he writes very new and modern music, he will not be understood by the faithful. And even much less will the parish priest or rector welcome him. But if he writes in the old nineteenth-century style, his music will not be valued by the scholar, because it will be found to be old-fashioned and senile as soon as it is written."

The great regret of the clarifier was that the document failed to provide for the long awaited and sovereign panacea, the

Graduale Simplex, a Latin one that would call for transliteration in any case. And musical settings for several voices, with or without accompaniment, could be performed by the choir (who else?), but no one was to be excluded. It fell short of forbidding, as an ancient Milwaukee syllabus had, TTBB choirs the use of SATB scores.

Succeeding instructions and their commentaries brought more of the same. The business of special melodies and rhythms for children was reiterated until it appeared that we were all to be kids again. They had done better to heed the late Zoltan Kodály who observed: "The poor quality of melody did not lead the children to good music, but rather to musical trash . . . a watered down substitute is *not* good enough to serve as learning material. Only the best is just good enough for our children." If anyone persisted, as I did, in teaching them Gregorian chant, the liturgist's knowing leer made him wonder how he could be so lucky as to be out on bail.

The admonition of February 17, 1967, that "the incorporation of incongruous melodies and texts, adapted from popular ballads, should be avoided," needed a loophole. An opening to bedlam came within the year from the Bishops' Advisory Committee:

> The liturgy by its nature normally presupposes a minimum of biblical culture and a fairly solid commitment of living faith. Often these conditions are not present. The assembly, or many of its members, are still in need of evangelization. The liturgy, which is not meant to be a tool of evangelization, is forced into a missionary role. *In these conditions the music problem is complex. On the one hand, music can serve as a bridge to faith, and therefore greater liberty in the selection and use of musical materials may be called for. On the other hand, certain songs normally called for in the climate of faith* (e.g. *psalms and religious songs*), *lacking such a climate, may create problems rather than solve them.*

With the postulates of the nature of liturgy and its music thus subverted, we got everything from recordings by Borodin to "Funny Girl"; musical backdrops for readings from Tennyson to Scott Fitzgerald. Richard Wagner and Leonard Bernstein may have bastardized the liturgy, but the experts bent it out of shape altogether. It was all unnecessary, for the liturgy had ever been missionary by being itself. And all of the farfetched new freedoms haven't worked because, as Flannery O'Connor said, freedom is of no use without taste.

Commentaries in the '70s, such as Louis Cyr's in *Concilium,*[3] keep the Church musician in a constant state of becoming. He is told that, since his basic training and attitude barely equip him to deal with the present situation, he may well doubt whether he is equal to the task facing him. Still, he must not excuse himself, hiding behind the "crisis in Church music," and become impotent because more is expected of him than he can give. For he has it on the happy word of the liturgist that we are at the beginning of a very creative phase in the realm of Church music. If he has no news of this creation, then no news is good news, and he need only peer with critical eye for every possible use of every possible music coming around the headland.

Meanwhile there is no more worry about proportion. Precelebration music must not be too short.[4] Motets must not be cut in half, nor combo or organist be cut off before their aleatrics have run their destined course. We may even cool our romance with relevance, lest having quit the past we find ourselves with nothing until the future arrives. People must not be tired by too much singing. All of those space and time problems can be met by properly adjusted electronics.

Certain honest and fundamental questions surfaced, questions which never seemed to have crossed the reformers' minds —such as: How do you transfer community music-making to the ecclesial community if there is no community music-making to begin with? Do you follow the American prescription of getting half-stoned in preparation? Do you succumb, like some, to the temptation of carefully adjusting amplification to talents not existing in the community with tapes, records, multimedia?

Ferdinand Haberl has observed that, while aesthetic appreciation might come about through mechanical reproduction, no true service of worship, no liturgy, will. Man should appear before God in prayer and song, he says, as a *homo ludens,* and not let himself be represented as an *apparatus ludens* through a *machina ludens.*

And at long last, someone else warns against compulsive

pandering to rock 'n' roll, lest canny youth suspect it is being used. There is indeed some evidence that it is quite the opposite tack that attracts the young, who, in Church at least, appear to want bread more than they want stones—even when they are "rolling."[5] It is crazy anyway to envy Pan the waves of folk who billow out of Madison Square Garden after a rock concert. That is not to say that fifty years from now the impact of the current genre will not be felt in Church music. It has cut across all political ideologies, and Chuck Berry predicted a long time ago that, after it had rolled right over Beethoven, it would likely rock into the maw of a cultural tolerance that preferred absorbing the music to standing around as a target to be flattened.

The great eruption of '55, the strong after-tremors of '64 and '67, they say, will not return. But the process of miscegenation has begun: fertilization with jazz, with country music, and even with the Lawrence Welk rock-waltz. The while the psychedelic light grows brighter, our hearing dimmer, and our voice boxes go the biological way of the appendix. There is no percentage in beating our breasts, or the air, about that. Nor in comparable circumstances has there ever been.

But the experts had better face up to the most basic questions of all if we are to be spared Armageddon a while longer: What is the philosophy of music? What *is* music? And can there be a functional music if by common definition it is no longer music but something else, however functional? One wishes they had read and taken to heart, some fifteen or twenty years ago, before the commotion began, Chesterton's parable, in *Heretics,* on the philosophy of light:

> Suppose that a great commotion rises in the street about something, let us say a lamp-post, which many influential persons desire to pull down. A grey-clad monk, who is the spirit of the Middle Ages, is approached on the matter, and begins to say, in the arid manner of the Schoolmen, "Let us first of all consider, my bretheren, the value of light. If light in itself be good . . ." At this point he is somewhat excusably knocked down. All the people make a rush for the lamp-post, the lamp-post is down in ten minutes, and they go about congratulating each other on their unmedieval practicality. But as things go on, they do

not work out so easily. Some people have pulled the lamp-post down because they wanted the electric light; some because they wanted darkness, because their deeds were evil. Some thought it not enough of a lamp-post, some too much; some acted because they wanted to smash municipal machinery; some because they wanted to smash something. And so there is war in the night, no man knowing whom he strikes. So gradually and inevitably, today, tomorrow, or the next day, there comes back the conviction that the monk was right after all, and that all depends on what is the philosophy of light. Only what we might have discussed under the gas-lamp, we must now discuss in the dark.

Music is like light, and Chesterton's parable is a striking illustration of what has happened to Church music at the hands of the experts.

~ VIII ~

WORDS AND MUSIC

It may be centuries before the Church has a body of music worth subjecting to an analysis of *Wort und Ton* in the Germanic tradition of Johner or Urbanus Bohm.[1] But for a start one might have hoped that the children of light would have been at least as circumspect as Gilbert and Sullivan or Rodgers and Hammerstein. If you want music, you had better pay some attention to the lyrics. Far from constituting any kind of challenge to musicians, it has seemed to me that too many of the new texts abhor music. And I keep thinking of the time someone asked Flannery O'Connor if she didn't think that too many English teachers discouraged their pupils from writing, and she replied that in her view they didn't discourage enough of them.

If that vast army of liturgical termites who fancy themselves composers ought to be discouraged, so should the suppliers of the texts they whittle away at. If the musician is to be challenged, he desperately needs: (a) the poetic verbalization basic to song and (b) a finalization of texts thus conceived. He has gotten neither. Only bids from men who, as St. Peter says, "are like dried up springs, like clouds blown along by a storm."

During the long Latin period of the Church, from St. Jerome onward, that twin consideration could be taken for granted. Translators were, from the point of view of language, generally faithful to what Eric Werner calls the Hebrew or Greek artistic prose of the Scriptures, even in those spots where it is seemingly folksy. The polished language of the Fathers of the Church, the texts ornamented by Gregorian, was not identical with the Latin vernacular of the period.[2] The literary value of the biblical books may vary, but the Vulgate was not produced by a committee. And if Luther's Bible underwent theological refinement, if the King James and Douay-Rheims were indeed the work of groups of scholars, these were of such superior mien that they bred a language.

A third Instruction of the Congregation of Divine Worship, on the "Correct Application of the Constitution on the Sacred Liturgy," (September 5, 1970) counseled that translations be done slowly, with the help of writers and poets. And that, because they were dealing with the mandated prayer of the Church, the tradition of anonymity be honored. Such was not the temper of the time, and the advice of the Congregation is, as they say, gone with some wind.

It is certainly all right for translators to draw upon the clarifications of ancient readings, as did Erasmus, but that is no excuse for their being banal. And one supposes that it is all right to have the 750 bishops of the English-speaking world comment on the "pastoral acceptability of the work," but that is no excuse for an end result that has the appearance of something hammered out in the manner of the paleographic selectivity of neums from variant manuscripts, productive of a kind of cant that never existed any place at any time. It is all a little like a motley group of *Sesame Street* characters placing here a letter, there a letter, and all of different colors.

In any case, the roster of ICEL does not exactly read like a literary *Who's Who*. The particular qualification for American membership seems to have been a deep involvement in the affairs of the Liturgical Conference (Diekman, McManus, Rotella).

A New York editor who checked the vocabulary of an interim breviary against a sixth-grade word list found every word there, except for proper names. Even if it were meant to be a book for children, children's books and children's music are best conceived by such craftsmen as Stevenson and Prokofiev. The hymns in this book, though, were deliberately un-hymned. The prose translations used had been the subject of an apology in the Foreword of the book from which they were taken.[3] It is a passing curiosity that the interim books are now on the ICEL people's and bishops' index, not because they are any better or worse than their own, but simply because they are not *theirs*. Now is not a season of tear-shedding for publishers, however, especially not for those who got in on the ground floor of the missalette rip-off, that wastrel bane of the good service book, of a possible service music tradition. (How would you feel if you had a monthly or bimonthly publication with a guaranteed sale of millions?)

One suspects that some of the textual juggling, like most of its musical counterpart, was done with an eye to the underrated common man. When Artemus Ward, the American humorist who so amused Lincoln, died in England, the *London Review* said that his genius "was like our church service, in one respect, that it is made to be understanded of the common people." The elegance of King James, it meant.

Of all the reformed liturgical books to have come out of Vatican II, the Roman Liturgy of the Hours has received most general and just acclaim, not only for its content but because it is also a literary reform of the unconscionable tampering with the psalter in the "new" breviary of Pius XII.[4] (He is said to have literally cried when its inadequacies were detailed to him, too late for approbation to be withdrawn.) The vernacular editions falter on the usual accounts, and more specially when they fail to adhere to the structure and content of the Latin model. The peculiar unction of the Latin liturgical texts may not be translatable for anyone who is used to them, except by someone like Dryden; but they came through better in the old St. Andrew's Missal and the English Dominicans' translation of the Roman breviary than they do in the consecrated banalities of today's liturgical patois.

Men need liturgy, and liturgy needs its own language. If liturgical Latin will no longer do, we shall have to invent one, in the manner of the Beatniks of a dozen years ago.

For reasons of economy or sheer independence, and surely of superior judgment, the hierarchies of Australia, England and Wales, Ireland and Scotland parted company with the rest of the ICEL brethren in issuing their own version of the Liturgy of the Hours. It was, in the view of many, a commendable step, and it avoids in some measure the old fashioned Sunday School book appearance of the American counterpart. There are few if any privately manufactured additions, and it is refreshing to encounter Newman and Knox and Hopkins in readings and hymns. There is an interesting note in the publishers' (Collins, London-Glasgow; E. J. Dwyer, Sidney; Talbot, Dublin) list of acknowledgements to the effect that "the practical needs of choral recitation prompted a number of revisions in the psalms and canticles," the revisions having been made with the agreement of the Grail.

One begins to wonder, anyway, about the exclusive use of the Grail psalms in Englished books. It is generally said that they are somehow more amenable to musical treatment than others. The only thing clear to me is that they were amenable to the anglicized version of the Gelineau psalms, which employed the sprung rhythm theory of the French Dominicans. That theory may be a Hebrew secret, but it is not an English secret, and the composer will surely opt for the pace, the measure, and the cadence of the new Latin psalter. It, in turn, so resembles the Vulgate, that any number of traditional vernacular versions might be put to use. The hymns are a comely lot, but the horological integrity of the Latin is most often lost. And the *preces* are wont to take care of a good many of the aspirations of the old private devotions, and most of the new cliches.

It is not likely that the Liturgy of the Hours will call for much music. The great monasteries of Europe, like Beuron and Downside, have already fashioned their own, and there will be no great common song to sift down to us; but the psalter and so many of the antiphons, versicles, and responses, are common to all of our liturgies. It is here that good composers will founder over the lack of poetic verbalization. I have no doubt that there is and will be no dearth of what some are pleased to call "contemporary settings," but as Eric Routley has said, the terrible thing about Victorian Church music was that it was all contemporary.

There is a further problem for the choirmaster, the planner of liturgy, and even for the "leader of song" and the missalette publisher, if they are serious about their business. That is that the pellucid, masterful unity of the old Office and Mass has been lost. Given the disposition of Mass readings over a period of three years and the annual rhythm of the Office, there was not much choice. But it remains to be seen whether the sacrifice was worth the effort.

The validity of the arrangement rests chiefly upon its proffering a wider acquaintance with the Scriptures. One may be allowed to wonder whether the additional pericopes, and the variant readings of the same events, will accomplish all that much. There was an admirable genius about the old selectivity, the unfailing yearly return to the mounting tensions, or the staying serenities. It bred a familiarity that the ternary cycles will be hard put to give. Repetition was indeed the mother of acquaintance, if not of study.[5]

Meanwhile the carefully tapestried attendant chants, both processional and intervenient, have been thrown all out of kilter.[6] The problems of clothing them with suitable melodies are staggering. It will not be the work of one generation, or ten. Because it is all too much to digest, the singing of the liturgical texts has been all but abandoned, and most congregations are thrown back upon shoddy substitutes offered in the lean hymn section of the average missalette—the nadir of liturgical impoverishment. If anyone were nervy enough to rely upon the vaunted *thesaurus* of the Church, he would have to own a battery of source books, and at least one of several indices or concordances to go with them.[7]

Meanwhile, at this quite late date, the editor of *Worship* is calling for joiners in an attempt to supply commissions. An American representative of ICEL sends a form letter to one of the most prominent French composers, asking him to try his hand at some English funeral responses. There is a deadline of some three months, and there will be no remuneration, unless someone decides that he is the lucky one. One of the truly contemporary Austrian composers revamps the vernacular writ of Holy Thursday so that he can turn out a suitable piece of music. A lecturer at a meeting of Church music editors at Princeton, New Jersey, is obliged to confess that he always looks at the music first, since he can always do something about the texts. And so the proliferation of unofficial texts continues, covering for the music we do not have, some composed, if not by Everyman, for Everytime.

The winner of a hymn contest sponsored by the 1976 Eucharistic Congress must first supply his own text, then revise it somehow to work in the sacred blood, though the theme is the bread of life. Nine out of ten of the dreadful attempts at Church composition that cross editors' desks are set to their own dreadful texts, like something called "Jan's Prayer."

While sparing ourselves the dreary largesse of specific examples of all this, the translators' senseless yen to improve on the original might be alluded to. Why, for example, after a millenium and a half, was it found necessary to add to the Nicene Creed? ("Died" was added.) Why tamper with the Gloria? In the December 1971 Bishops' Committee's Newsletter, the new English text, prepared by the International Consultation on English Texts (ICET), an ecumenical group, and proposed by the Catholic ICEL, was pronounced "both singable and recitable." It *reproduced,* they said, "in a new idiom, this very ancient and venerable hymn." It was a new idiom all right, but even less singable and recitable than the much caricatured interim "you-who" version: "This ancient piece is poetry in prose, an emotionally tinged outpouring of praise. Such lyrics do not avoid repetition, they favor it. Moreover, a grouping of lines into symmetrical patterns easily occurs. The official Latin text, just republished in the *Ordo Missae* without change, is characterized by groupings in threes. The new translation has suppressed this in the second part and obscured it in the first, in the interest apparently of economical and more rational expression. Of course, the shift from the third person at Gloria in Excelsis to the second person at Laudamus te leaves the nature of *te* unexplained. So the translators moved the vocative Domine Deus up to the front to make that clear. But did anybody ever doubt about who was meant? Does poetry worry about such things"?[8]

The same sort of approach, call it rational or witless, turns the succinct, happy sense of the responses to the Preface verses into pedestrian declarations. The latest official prefatory music fares no better. If ever there was a simple and clear example of tone painting, it was the brief melisma over *Sursum Corda.* I can still hear all those patriarchs soaring to the heights like ancient eagles. The new music, a pale kind of chant subversion with its descending motif over "lift," would give their portly counterparts the sound and effect of a blimp deflating. It's just as well that it is rarely sung.[9]

The ICET-ICEL Gloria, of course, is still with us,[10] and it may seem paranoid both to complain about texts and to plead for their finalization. But the music will have to wait for both literary restoration and finalization. Great orchestral music did not arise until the distribution of the instruments was settled, and composers of music for the Church have long since tired of seeing their efforts outdated every few years.[11] The latest word from ICEL, to which it is difficult to give a vote of confidence anyway, is that that body will be an ongoing instrument of revision.

Before the vernacular barrier was ever broken, an organization called Friends of the English Liturgy (FEL) was reared in and about Chicago. It was engaged chiefly in experimentation about what might be in both rite and music, and has by now become a self-styled interdenominational venture much concerned about copyright violation.[12] What we desperately need is a brand new *Friends* of the English liturgy. Real ones, this time.

~ IX ~

PRELUDES

The journey to 1970 from, say, 1950, seems now like meandering through the Olde Curiosity Shoppe. After the Assisi Congress in 1956, Bishop Wright expressed relief over what he described as its disposition to retain and defend the use of Latin in the liturgy.[1] It was the heyday of the breakthrough to vernacular rituals, and he thought it safe to guess that permission would be sought to read the Epistles and Gospels in the language of the people without reciting them in Latin first. Petitions were indeed filed in Rome, but in receiving liturgical leaders after the Congress, Pius XII remarked that it would be "superfluous to call to mind once more that the Church has great motives for firmly insisting on the absolute obligation of the priest celebrating Mass to use Latin," and also for the Gregorian chant being done in the Church's tongue.

Someone "discovered" that there were ancient churches with altars that faced the people, when all they were doing was facing the east. Colonel Ross Duggan's *Amen* heralded pictures of such, of Communion in the hand, of the "bearers of the paschal lamb, previously cooked on a crossed spit." Father Ellard, crusading for evening Mass, quoted Romeo to Juliet, "Shall I come to you at evening Mass?" And Father Nutting, the Anglican convert recently deceased, campaigned not for English but for great English, warning nonetheless that the "use of English does not make foolish people wise or mumbling clergymen unmumbling."

It should be reported that the American Church music com-

munity was *not* fighting any rearguard action. It was not mobil-
ized to do anything but wait, ready to try to do what it was told.
Its experience with the first several years of the new Holy Week
liturgy should have prepared it for the greatest possible confusion, even though the vernacular had not compounded musical
problems then. No official music had reached our shores, and
as late as February 28, 1952, the best information I could pass
out was that "sometime in the coming months we will receive,
in small quantities, a new Holy Week book, and it would seem
unwise to make an investment prior to a perusal of it." The
improvisations, published and unpublished, were legion, and,
musically, the great week has been pretty much a jumble ever
since.

It was clear that we had lost the mighty *Vexilla Regis;* and that
because Matins and Lauds were not to be anticipated, Tenebrae
was out, except in the morning or on Wednesday night in cathedrals where the Mass of the Chrism would be celebrated. Ordinary folk had been wont to fill the churches where those services
were held, and not just for the climactic *strepitus.* (Tenebrae lives
on in a few Anglican establishments of high calling, and in one
or the other other Catholic revivals in Edinburgh, Scotland, and
Toronto, Ontario. It is probably better attended than the non-
sectarian New Year's Eve Tre Ore in Omaha.)

In 1963, Joseph Jungmann was still calling for balance, decry-
ing the heat of the battle which engendered such remarks as:
"Church choirs and polyphonic high Masses must fall into
decay." He put it this way: "Congregational singing must be
admitted because the liturgy is the Church's worship; but the
potentialities of Church musical art must also be admitted because the liturgy is God's service." Few besides the Lutherans
had not forgotten that. He was thinking of festal occasions
everywhere and of representative churches in large cities any
time, where "Church music would predominate, especially that
of recent centuries." This was the Austrian and south German
in him, though I have found similar thinking as far afield as
Newfoundland.

Complaints began to be heard from abroad. The Church
Music Association of England submitted that the approach to
the problem of musical participation in England and Wales

might possibly be very different from that in other countries, that "in particular any attempt to impose musico-liturgical forms which neither correspond with English cultural traditions nor take into account the traditions of the Church of England or other Christian bodies in this country would be mistaken and impracticable." They considered the traditional Latin sung Mass a form whose unity would be impaired by the introduction of liturgical texts sung in the vernacular: that a *music* of the vernacular liturgy would develop only through an established and accepted *spoken* vernacular liturgy.

The distinguished German composer, Hermann Schroeder, lamented a garbled vernacular form of the Pater which respected neither the characteristics of the language nor the Gregorian structure. Other species of German composition, born of the circumstance of hurried reforms, were "chiefly remarkable for being musically rudimentary, impoverished and over simplified." He spurned the promise of vernacular *propria* while melodies for a typical edition hadn't even been composed; and he regarded with horror "those who were advocating a so-called *Graduale Simplex* which entirely disregarded the liturgical *ordo* of the authentic Gregorian melodies, and which was thought of, in any case, merely as a future source of vernacular adaptations." With their eyes on pie in the sky, American commentators were calling for an ever-expanding use of antiphonal psalmody.

Schroeder said that in the matter of popular song, religious or secular, history and experience proved that only rhythmic settings had ever been successful,[2] and that the melodies approved by the "territorial authority" up until then had been marked by a frenzy of supply and demand, whereas authentic art required a condition of calm leisure. Only the CIMS appeal to the Holy See to bring together the best composers in the world to elucidate the problems and to facilitate experimental composition, were it acted upon, might surmount the running dilettantism, the commercialism of editors who had no regard for quality.

Jacques Chailley, professor of music history at the Sorbonne, was dismayed at his country's frantic attempt to "kill silence." Even musicians had little of it left—that silence "which is the palette on which they paint their sounds." A correspondent equated the old organ Mass with silence, and thus music with nothing. But there was warm approval of the directives of the French hierarchy that specified obligatory ministers' chants, and that declared that pastoral necessity must not serve as a pretext for either mediocrity or platitude, and that the spirit of the Council had been one of balance. *Nova et vetera:* a search for the music of our times, fidelity to the patrimony of the past. For that, the singing prelate of Pamiers[3] said, was the history of music itself. Compare that with these weather vanes out of *Aim,* published by the Paluch Missalette: "Through trial and error I have discovered that the best way to find competent song leaders is to seek out women and men who belong to either the Sweet Adelines or the Barbershop Quartets,"—at least as sexist as the Sistine Choir. Not those worthies, nor anyone else, could guess that in August of 1975, the Liturgical Conference, still refusing to grow up, would request the National Conference of Bishops to remove all sexist language in official prayer—like "shed for you and all men," "for us men and our salvation," "pray brethren." It couldn't have come up with that if it knew any Latin, or Old English, or new English.

"We have seven song leaders in our parish. Each of them is excellent. Not one of them can sing."

"On that Sunday, we always use the new hymn as the opening hymn. On the following Sunday we use it as the Offertory hymn, and the next Sunday as the closing hymn. We would use it a couple of times on the following Sunday if it remained in the book." The liturgy, as the experts say, is ambivalent.

In 1967, the bishops weren't fast enough with the new Canon of the Mass, and the editors of *Liturgy* wrote: "It is absolutely necessary that there be no obstruction or delay in granting us its use. Some of us still care about communion with the Roman See. Every unreasonable delay (like the present one, which we hope will be over before you receive this issue), every rejection of a reasonable request, sets our cause back. This is not a threat. It is a lament and a demand." By opening night of the Kansas City Liturgical Week, announced as "Sights and Sounds of People," the Conference persons were less strident. The *National Catholic Reporter* entitled its release "Kandy-Kolored Happening, Baby," and went on to say that at the end of the evening "we had the basis of community . . . when it was all over, two bishops were singing about big yellow balloons and nobody giggled." That was before an alternative service to explore the feasibility of experimental worship through the behavioral sciences, but after Trudy Califano had cheered them on with her reading of "The Velveteen Rabbit" during the Liturgy of the Word in the Mass of the Future.

Nearer home, there were three such Masses during a provincial meeting that was supposed to be as pristine as the Franciscan Chapter of the Mats: Epistles and Gospels from Teilhard's *Hymn of the Universe,* Sandburg's *Timesweep,* and the Declaration of Independence. The announced readers have since declared *their* independence. In the context of the time, it was all tame enough, and apparently beyond the reach of the local "territorial authority." All he did, with a show of petulance, was refuse to celebrate with them.

Diocesan lists of approved music, and futile choir days to demonstrate it, flourished. They were mostly alike. Montreal asked for a copy of ours, and a Chicago friend, where the sung Latin Mass had been banned, wrote that the only criteria used there were: (a) Is it on the market? and (b) Has it been approved in another diocese? All this was only good for interim texts, of course. Some publishers made a little hay during early sunbursts; others, with reams of one-shot music on their shelves, understandably went broke. Church music purchased is likely to be the fare for at least a generation, and an early indication of the general debility of the Catholic conscience was the most wholesale epidemic of pirating and copyright violation in history.

Church music manuals, guidelines, and hymnals proliferated, too. Of the latter, Benziger's and the *New St. Basil's* were too good and too soon. Arthur Reilly's notable *Pius X* book never displaced the old *St. Gregory,* even in his own store, and that sterling gentleman confided that it was a matter of considerable regret that his Church music ventures were not as successful as his political ones. Careful commissions were cautioning: "When and if you do decide to purchase new hymnals, please keep in mind further changes in translations, expected in two to five

years." The genial Omer Westendorf's widely used and up-
dated *People's Mass Book* would not save his great World Library
of Sacred Music (WLSM) experiment from insolvency.
McLaughlin & Reilly is no more, and hardly anything of its
catalog survives in Summy-Birchard, as little enough of WLSM
survives in Paluch. It still carries the *People's Mass Book*, but
doesn't advertise it against its missalette *Geschäft*. Large
amounts of the rest were sold for their paper weight.

None of the many published guidelines were binding, and
that is just as well, for the section on the organ in the Liturgical
Conference's manual proffered all sorts of unprofessional advice—a pitch for the exclusive use of eight-foot diapason stops,
persistent admonitions against mutations and mixtures in accompanying either congregation or choir (the manner of accompanying both was deemed precisely the same), and a puritan prohibition of reeds.

An Iowa commission listed seven conditions under which the
bishop might permit guitar accompaniments at Mass: It must be
for young people, in church, and not be called "hootenanny."
The instrumentalists were to be competent, and not placed in
the sanctuary or the pulpit. In the late 60s, one no longer heard
of the sanctuary, but of the "presbyterium," loosely defined as
the area used by the celebrating clergy. When the altar rails
and/or Communion stations were abandoned, there was nothing left for guitarists and lady lectors to stay out of.

An Ohio commission had kinder thoughts about the Bernstein "Mass" than Berlinski did, citing one segment as the ideal
equivalent of the Gospel acclamation, although it was "not suggested that every parish manage that sort of thing every Sunday." But by then most music commissions had either inte-
grated or disintegrated into liturgical commissions, and the
national federation of those commissions began to show some
of the muscle flexed by the Liturgical Conference before it went
the way of Elizabeth Bentley's Red Network at its Milwaukee
meeting. The Music Advisory Board rated an episcopal representative, and the CMAA lost its chief reason for existence. For
that, it had only its intransigent elements to blame.

An offshoot, the Composers' Forum for Catholic Worship,
based in Sugar Creek, Missouri, received a formal letter of rec-

ognition and encouragement from the Bishops' Committee on the Liturgy. Such letters were sent elsewhere too, and they may be only a token of what Patrick Moynihan called "benign neglect." Something more than that, more than mere competence and shoestring financial operations, had been needed for over a decade. The Forum's offerings reach a relatively few subscribing members, and have not generated a demand that would warrant general publication.

Denouement: In November 1973, the National Conference of Catholic Bishops accepted a proposal to petition the apostolic see to permit in this country the liturgical institution of ministers of sacred music, alongside the lay ministries of reader, acolyte, and catechist. So much shadow, so little substance.

There is a story about a preview of the *Missa Normativa*, enacted in Rome for the assembled cardinals' and bishops' amazement. To simulate the average parish, they took the part of the congregation, Cardinal Tisserant that of the celebrant. The recessional hymn was a French version of "Nearer My God to Thee." Bishop Wright is said to have turned to Cardinal Brown and asked what he thought of the whole thing. Brown thought that the closing hymn, at least, was appropriate. Wright asked why, and Brown replied: "Isn't that what they sang when the *Titanic* went down?"

FUGUES

Fugued right out of the preludes. The pattern is everywhere the same, here and abroad. A church in New Haven advertises itself in the Yellow Pages as "The Encountered Church," but what one encounters is mostly foolishness or frustration. The reservoirs of good will evident during the prelude have dried up. The trite, perennial optimists still tell us that if choirs had stuck to their basic function of singing the people's parts for two solid years, they could have spent the next thirteen catching up. The people who tried that, in a desperate and noble effort to shore up their parishes against the amusical forces unleashed by liturgists—CCD or YCS, motherhouse or monastery—have lost their musical souls, if not their jobs. The more cautious optimist begins to surmise that we have turned a corner. The only corner turned that I can see is an economic one: pastors and parishes are paying a good deal more for a good deal less.

Hear, then, some thematic material for the fugue. You might expect it to be heavily slanted, and it is: not a single encouraging report is omitted, but much oppositive intelligence is. These accounts have not been gathered by any research institute, nor even in the manner in which one goes about firming up a master's thesis, an indiscriminate peddling of fixed questionnaires for a random sampling of nothing. They are based not on hearsay but on experience, and before one has followed the recurring motif very long, one might well wish one were dealing only with the standard dictionary's second definition of fugue: "an interval of flight from reality."

Chicago, for example, can be described as dismal: only a handful of places where good music is occasionally performed —Christmas and Easter, or at best once a month at the old church where my grandparents were married.

The reactions of local parishioners are interesting, and certainly understandable: Rose's church managed to keep a choir of sorts that stuck to simple arrangements of hymns like "What the World Needs Now Is Love." That didn't hold the young people's interest, older members soon gave up, and Rose has gone into business. Anne learned from the pulpit one Sunday that her boys' choir, representing an arduous and successful parish-school effort of twenty years, was to be abandoned. She is still organist at the church and at home weddings, where she can play quite a lot if the J. P. is late. In Quebec, there are still one or two choirs, but in Chestnut Hill, Virginia's nerves are frayed by a female voice singing "If I Had the Wings of a Dove" throughout Communion. So she went to Italy four or five times to hear "Koombayah" *a cappella,* a folk Mass in the catacombs, and Holy Week at St. Peter's.

Sister Thomasine refuses to play any longer without remuneration, her family and community having put a small fortune into her education. She played at the cathedral on Good Friday, but can't afford American Guild of Organists conventions anymore, even when they are held locally. But there are some four or five churches in the metropolitan area that have good music, one with Vespers.

A little over a year ago, another Virginia submitted to total frustration, writing: "I don't have the slightest intention of ever going back into Church music, or Church either, for that matter. If mood music is required for the Eucharist, let them install a good sound system. The new Lutheran Liturgy, sung fairly well by my Lutheran choir, bombed with the Church people, and didn't even get to the kids it was written to impress. If I could take the type of music the World Action singers use, I wouldn't bother to get out of bed on Sundays. If I go, it's during the week, when it's quiet. The pitiful Catholic choirs that accompany the Mass on TV, after Oral Roberts, make you want to weep. So for me, nothing has changed since my last session at Union where the consensus was: Church music has to go where the Church goes. And where is the Church going? The Roman statements have obliterated decent music here, the Episcopalians and Lutherans are juggling, the Gospel singers are still doing their own thing, and nobody else believes in religion anyway."

Ralph was not booted out of his cathedral, but resigned on principle since that was what the "diggers" wanted. A cathedral choir director, he had planned a Schubert Mass for a bishop's jubilee. When there was a fuss about that (not on the part of the bishop) he switched to an incontrovertible Mass by Erb, and soon found that Schubert was not the crux. He thinks that things like the Buccaneer Music Festivals offer some hope. Good choral training and taste have filtered down to the public high schools from college and university, and a lot of Catholic kids are singing anything from des Prés to Ginastera.

Lou asks whether I can imagine her asking for a Gregorian *Requiem* when her husband died, and getting it. A neighboring convert's choir had recently sung a Gregorian Mass at the request of the high-school Latin class. But the wholly uninspired, unsinging ditties they have the children sing for their First Communion are shocking. She asked the cathedral organist, who supplies a Latin Mass a month, what the Baptist hymnals on the shelf were for. The better to dress up their unadorned extracts in the missalettes. In her own church, Lou manages notable propriety—Gregorian, Bruckner, Palestrina, Aichinger, Gounod, Holy God.

Sister Muriel felt like a foreigner when she came to Philadelphia. She hadn't any bilingual groups—Spanish or Lithuanian —to work with, and there were no Saturday evening Masses. (In general, it seems a fair judgment that congregational singing fares best in ethnic parishes.) However, the Confraternity of Christian Doctrine supplied practically all of the smaller churches with guitar groups. There was hardly any chant, and while she didn't think Peloquin was much help to the humbler churches, or the unhumble for that matter, she didn't know what she would do with *her* thesis on "The Aesthetic Experience Derived from Synthesizers and Computers" either.

Ireland is lucky, D'Nell says, for it is still mostly quiet at Mass. In the larger cities, the organists are poor and the singing less than enthusiastic. The Galway Cathedral maintains a men and boys choir, and the organist prays that the bishop will outlive her. There is the Van Dessel Choir of seventy voices at Dundalh, trained by and named after the late Flemish organist. It sang in Rome during the canonization of Oliver Plunkett, but not at St. Peter's, where it was suggested that the singing should consist of little Irish hymns. "Nearer My God to Thee," the Protestant staple for funerals, has become the favorite for Catholic weddings. (A friend of mine has sometimes administered the new rite of Anointing of the Sick to couples about to be married.)

Back in Ohio, there is not much for faithful D'Nell's own choir to do because they have to use the Sunday missalettes for words and music. Weddings, and even funerals, are nightmares; a refusal of outlandish requests only drives the bidders to those who don't attend the locally sponsored seminars on wedding and funeral music; and the Protestant organists blame the Catholic Church for the stuff they must now put up with. A sermon on conjugal love turns out to be a tape from *Fiddler on the Roof,* and for the rest there is a pervasive pattern of sundry make-ups for big occasions: appeals for choirs to participate in essaying the Gloria from the *Missa Zamba* (thus simulating congregational singing) and a catching-up to the liturgical propriety of Joe Wise.

In a western diocese, the bishop remarks that the music situation is infinitely better than it used to be—whatever that was. A non-Catholic doctor who serves on the Music Commission and edits its respectable newsletter guesses that they do indeed bat around .300 in the matter of creditable choirs, balanced liturgies, and congregational response. The folk Mass is everywhere. Some are good, most are awful, but some people seem to get religion from guitars, the ultimate apologetic. The neighboring metropolis still goes the old route of the professional quartet, sometimes supported by a volunteer choir. The cathedral choir of about forty voices, plus a large instrumental group and knowing rector, sings twice every Sunday, and an appreciative congregation sings its heart out and occasionally applauds. Community and communion.

The Southern Baptist bent, predicted by Paul Henry Lang and reported by Leo Rosten after the Fourth International Eucharistic Congress, is in full swing. Cardinal Suenens leads

18,000 charismatics, rock-guitars and all, in St. Peter's; and in St. Paul, Minnesota, 4,500, charged up by thunderous sermonizing, drum, and smoke, break away now and again to buy soft drinks to quench the inner fire. Two and a half hours of this, but only ninety minutes get on the cassettes they can purchase in the lobby when they depart. At the two-hour finale of the 1975 Liturgical Week in Princeton, the conferees were "filled with such joy" after the final hymn that they called the Archbishop of Halifax and his ministers back into the hall for prolonged applause. Maybe curtain calls are what we have needed all along. It was heady stuff for the archbishop, who didn't participate in the more modest weekend affair of his Newfoundland neighbors. A *National Catholic Reporter* report of similar euphoria in a West End San Antonio parish is much overdrawn. The mariachis were better than I heard in Mexico, the singing was mostly choir with but mild congregational assists, and during Communion there was participation by listening to a bland Anglo trio. It all lasted less than an hour.

In Baltimore, the number of priests distributing Communion has been increased to cut down the length of the Mass, and the cathedral bulletin carried this warning: "The behavior of some of our younger teen-agers in and around and after the folk Mass in the undercroft leaves much to be desired . . . a number of youngsters waiting for their parents or friends have simply made the area a place to carry on such boisterous conduct as to be heard in the sanctuary. Other youngsters do not attend Mass at all but roam around or have a smoke in the rest rooms, often leaving behind graffiti which makes interesting reading indeed. Were I their headmaster, I would at least suggest that they not wear their school jackets during such capers, lest their chauvinism redound to a bad name for the academic institution they represent. If the situation does not improve, something stronger than my admonition will have to be done."

The dancing, swaying, and hand-clapping is not all of the ecstatic, improvised genre of the revival tent.[1] It has become a liturgical occupation. However much it might be rooted in the medieval cathedral of Toledo, the ancient calisthenics of the Grail, or the pedagogical device of Gregorian eurhythmics, it flits from continent to continent with Gloria and Deiss, inspiring much too hefty high-school girls to do a kind of dance of the battleships on TV while their chorus swoons to *Stille Nacht.* An American organist advertises the Messiaen *Nativity* with or without choreography, and Jean Langlais, who played part of the premiere, says that is crazy. There are all of those psalmic references to dancing with joy before the Lord, of course, but I fancy that dancing with joy before the Lord is Carleton Fisk rounding first base in the last half of the ninth in the sixth game of the '75 World Series.

Publishers have their own little fugue. "Parish priests, choirs, schools, laity—have you got the new *Jubilate Deo* record?" For two and a half pounds, or $4.95 American, you can learn *Kyrie 16, Gloria 8* and the *O Salutaris* all over again. The "Total Worship Program" for '76 includes a seasonal missalette and a 256-page bound hymnal to be revised every three years so that you can have an up-to-date music resource. In view of ICEL's plans to revise translations, prepare additional texts and music—one cannot afford to take chances. (ICEL recently held its first worldwide meeting in Singapore. A computer had told them that that was the Committee's geographic center, but not that the delegates from New Zealand and Tanzania couldn't come.) Advertising the late Jan Kern's settings of all the new Prefaces, the Gregorian Institute of America asks, "Are you less than pleased with the ones in the new sacramentary?" (Kern's are unquestionably better.) And adds: "The time has come for the Catholic Church to have a real hymnal—watch out missalettes!"

Catholic publishers say that the expense to pastor and parish of pew materials has made almost impossible whatever other music purchases might have to be made. Anyway, there isn't much in their catalogs worth buying. An Austrian radio competition for new Mass settings has gone two years without awarding a first prize. Jazz Masses there and elsewhere are liable to be German adaptations of "Erie Canal" or spirituals,—hardly indigenous.

In Jersey, Jeff tries to gather enough money to rebuild his church's centennial organ. The choir of thirty is very much alive, and so is the parish program, although there is the usual worry about how long one can brave the tide. Material used is first-rate, the advent of the vernacular having served as a proper excuse to delete a substantial amount of old Latin war-horses. Some eight or ten of the membership have asked to study Gregorian on the side, and they have got back to a Latin Mass once a month. On occasion they manage to finance special sacred concerts professionally augmented.

The best run-of-the-mill parish Mass Louise had heard was a mariachi one at Carmel: two good guitars, two good trumpets. Campus ministries had been devastated and choirs destroyed by atrocious attempts at congregational composition by well-meaning music students. And the most unlikely twentieth-century contrafactum was the Polish church's setting of "Danny Boy."

In Cambridge, the exemplary and musically formidable forces at St. Paul's are still in the saddle, and so is Gregorian chant. The choir school is open, though the grammar school it occupies has closed. The diocese pays half the cost of the operation in recognition of its burgeoning contributions to the area. Besides alumni-run programs in other parishes, it sponsors an extensive training and certification program. Twenty-eight out of forty-two organ candidates (already playing in parishes) knew enough to begin elementary lessons—that is, they could read the bass clef—and twelve of these finished the first hurdle of an ongoing program.

Ted Marier and his abettors have to raise the other half of the operational costs. The word is around that the diocese is going bankrupt and they can't plan more than a year ahead. The Catholic University has made overtures toward a transplant, but the suggestion of a modest $100,000 budget drives administrators to distraction. So that Ted teaches only a summer chant course, for which there seems to be some demand.

In Los Angeles, the heyday of the choral Mass at old St. Joseph's is over. Paul Salamunovich still has a full liturgy at St. Charles, and St. Basil's, with the backing of cardinal and pastor against sometimes witless curates. But there is a dearth of boys, due, he says, to a lack of parental interest and responsibility.

In the Bronx, at St. Philip Neri, the Welch Chorale carries on as heretofore. Jim Welch works in the school now with student lectors and whatnot, helps with high-school musicals, attracts new blood.

Out in the Midwest George is fifty now, well-groomed and grey. Except for his job at the parish, he has pulled out of the music scramble, including the AGO. The program there is seeded in the grade school and flowers on the adult parish level. He has a boys' and men's choir, a girls' choir, and a mixed adult choir comprised of an amazing 62 percent of parish-school alumni. His school religion classes and evening Bible classes give form to the matter. The choirs sing both Saturday evening and Sunday; English mostly, but also Latin and chant, which especially interest the high-school element. A neighboring city parish, one of three or four deserving of mention in the metropolitan area, got superlatives for fine Masses and Vespers in a rather English tradition. He wasn't too sure about another church, of good enough repute, where the director was teaching the kids yoga for breathing purposes, except that it seemed to work, for they manage a sound big enough to fill the Cologne Cathedral.

The seminary is almost entirely English, with instruction in congregational singing but no chant. Seminarians in the choir and their combos go out into parishes on Sundays to spread the good news. St. Agnes is served by its own choir and a city-wide chorale and symphony which do the Viennese classics three Sundays a month. That seems to wash better than contemporary material and/or Renaissance polyphony, the pastor says, and indeed the sung Masses are crowded. There is also a small chant schola. Latin is adhered to, and the service is currently picked up each Sunday by Minnesota PBS. Crispin still has a choir of twenty or thirty and, without pretending to know anything about it, swears at the dearth of good vernacular music.

"Strike the Shepherd"—when Father Brunner died, George Z. was fired. Some lady with a guitar took over the boys, the men joined a competent organist in a neighboring parish, and the whole business petered out within the year. George had been preparing the Ralph Vaughn Williams *Mass in G Minor* for Christmas when the end came. That spring, the Communist Yugoslav Military Chorus came to town, and in an unannounced program sang it for the public, with Gregorian VII as encore. Duties at a large Catholic university, which George dubs the greatest secular campus in town, prevented his accepting the directorship of a particularly well-known, but now disbanded, boy choir. So he tries to bring music into his history classes and into his psychoanalytic study of the emperor Tiberius. Of his offhand remarks about Christian music, one student said, "What's the sense in that, when they tell us in the School of Theology that Christ was not an historical personage?" But there are one or two Gregorian Masses on campus each week, sandwiched in between the gung-ho guitars, and Ph.D.s carry on their research projects at the expense of a generation of dummies, he says.

In St. Louis, the seminary music program has finally been wrested from student control. There still is no chant, but they manage the *Veni Creator* for ordinations. There are Latin rumblings at the university and another parish, and at the cathedral a large music program goes on apace, mostly in English but with as heartening an aside as I have observed—eight or ten priests meet at Mario Salvador's house a couple of late hours each week for serious practice. They augment the men and boys for the larger liturgies and sing the chrism Mass on Holy Thursday. They, and the older men, remember some of the chant Propers.

Malcolm, busy now as department head at the university, can't answer all of the calls he gets to advise and consent. Anyway, he resents the notion that because he is black, he might be expected to equate blacks' musical perception with the insular thrust to the Spiritual and the Gospel song: a thrust that considers a traditional education of centuries in this hemisphere, evinced by Jose Nunes Garcia, William Grant Still, Chevalier de Saint-Georges and others, as something foreign and unethical. There were some good things in town, in the Italian community, where a Canadian held forth, and at St. Martin de Porres, where there were vestiges of a former repertoire. (What would they ever do with those stacks of Dominican *Graduales?*) And some Palestrina is left at the cathedral, though one would have thought from the organist's wild address to the AGO Quarterly a couple of years ago that the Roman Church was well past that sort of thing. And First Communion classes in another parish might just as well be singing chant as the trashy tunes imposed on them.

It's not just the jazz idiom, which everyone seems to think is passing. And it's not the guitars and percussion, which certainly are not passing. While they are hopeless for congregational accompaniment, they are suitable enough for the small, intimate performing groups which constitute the new choir and the new front drop. It's just that for lack of planning, lack of thinking, lack of taste, the fugue isn't going anywhere. At its best, it is inoffensive, and rarely does one hear it at its best. Too often it might be on the subject of a letter Erasmus wrote to Nicholas Varius from Basel, on September 26, 1526: "In olden times the Corybants drove people into a frenzy with the din of timbrels and flutes. That kind of noise has an amazing power for arousing emotions. But the drums we use today sound even more horrible with their noisy anapestic or pyrrhic beat. These we Christians now use in war instead of trumpets, as if it were not enough to be filled with courage, but one had also to become frenzied. Did I say war? We use them at weddings, too, and on holidays, and in churches. When they hear that wild, noisy rhythm, young girls rush out into the streets and the new bride does a dance. This is what sparks a holiday celebration: it is the height of fun when all day long throughout the streets wild confusion reigns, worse than that of the Corybants. In my opinion, this is the instrument used for celebrating holidays in hell, if they have any down there. Plato thinks the type of music enjoyed by a community is very important. What would he say if he heard such music among Christians?"[2]

TWICE THROUGH
THE RUBBLE

The Late Forties

Should the writer of these pages seem a trifle exercised, it ought to be recorded that he was ever thus. For all that one swore by the charter right through Vatican II, ferreting out its proper afterclap was no easy matter. At least principle held firm, and faulty or misguided application still stuck to principle.

A round of Sunday High Masses in New York City—one could make five or six—in the mid-forties was a pretty desultory experience. Bill McDonald was carrying on with the support of Father Ford in the neighborhood of Columbia University, and Jim Welch was getting started at St. Philip Neri in the Bronx. While in New York one could always find surcease by dropping into any one of a half dozen Anglican churches, for the Roman ones pretty much reflected what was going on across the rest of the country. Mostly there was an unhinged and disavowedly new Cecilian school, fresh off the American church presses: Yon, Carnevali, René Becker and Alfred Schehl, Rossini and Gruber near the top. Omer Westendorf had not yet introduced the general public to what were comparably exciting contemporary developments in Europe.[1]

I remain grateful for the opportunity of a sabbatical afforded me in 1949, and though I was sent to Rome I mostly played hookey there. I was, in any case, past acquiring the churchly Roman stamp in matters musical, and wary enough of that Roman club. There is no sense in impugning an Alma Mater camaraderie, but blinkers often seem to be a motherly graduation gift.

In 1949 such a trip was an excursion through the rubble of the war, and it was perhaps not a vintage year. While music was still a part of life and part of the Church's worship, there were more pressing interests. In Cologne, only the proud Dom reared its towers to survey the ruins. One Sunday morning in Munich, I heard the Beethoven *Missa Solemnis* in the Frauenkirche, which was badly shot up. The organ was gone, but the gallery had been sufficiently repaired with temporary materials to support the singers and instrumentalists. The pillars that raised the great arches seemed like unfinished lumber, most of the floor was dirt, and the windows were boarded up. In the damp cold of the morning, it took a while for the orchestra to play in tune, for the only warmth came from packed rows of worshipers, parents occasionally moving their children into random shafts of sunlight; censer smoke whiffed through the drafts like snow sprites. Even then, when I was much inclined to look askance at what I deemed the lack of liturgical integrity in pieces like the Beethoven or the Bach *B-minor,* the garb seemed to fit the body far better than the musical smock thrown about the liturgy today. Twenty-five years later I would wonder a bit, in the *Stefans-Dom* in Vienna, that the Agnus Dei of the Beethoven *Mass in C* didn't even succeed in covering the long procession of communicants.

Paris was not then a city of light, and there were only dim if pleasant echoes of choristers in Notre Dame. Switzerland was not suffering, and carried an air of braggadocio about having stayed out of the war. One night, in a heated exchange of simplifications, an American colonel friend slapped his drink on the bar and declared: "Of course you stay out of wars! Who the hell wants your country?" (Almost everybody.) There were itinerant bands of singers from the Vienna Opera earning a few centimes with worn-out potpourris of Straussian operetta; and there, in Lucerne, was the unalloyed satisfaction of the near perfect High Mass in the Hofkirche under J. Baptiste Hilber.

Monte Cassino was crushed to the size of giant ant hills, and Santa Chiara in Naples was a shell. Rome, which hadn't even the telltale pockmarks of Paris, was nonetheless without electricity twice a week, short of hot water—if not hot air—and subjected to frequent strikes, of which it must be said that they rarely lasted more than a couple of hours. Of all this, perhaps, the Church music situation was symptomatic, though one soon suspected that not within anyone's memory had the vaunted Roman tradition equaled that of England, and it was quite clear how Father Finn could and should have gone away running in international competition.

At the Pontifical Academy, Dom Desroquettes was initiating a new and not very well grounded generation into the mysteries of Solesmes rhythm with the sweeping strokes of a violinist and in an exhalation of *un'-due-tre,* tick-tock, tick-tock. Monsignor Zehrer, an Austrian, took all comers through a large repertoire of male voiced arrangements of polyphony not meant to be thus deranged, covering much, finishing nothing. Iginio Anglès gave the place stature by sheer force of his own personal reputation. It was said that he didn't follow the Solesmes trail as a musicologist, but he had been pretty severe with Peter Wagner for being severe with Solesmes. (The sage of Fribourg had not been allowed to peruse the manuscripts there until years after his studies had been finished, when Dom Gajard welcomed him.)

In the churches, there were few forays into polyphony. The chant was mostly *bel canto,* and there wasn't much else beyond Perosi and Refice.[2] The latter had returned from an ill-conceived tour of the United States to find Dominic Bertolucci at his post in St. Mary Major. It was rumored that there had been some dissent over his billing his recruits as "the Vatican Choir," and that that was why the American hierarchy hadn't come to his rescue. But if the American bishops were approached at all, they probably would have had to take the same dim view as Columbia Concerts, called late in the day. The thing was so loosely organized that only something like a Ford Foundation grant could have saved it. We crisscrossed each other in the West in the fall of 1947, and I always felt sorry for the *bambini* who were marched about resolutely while some of the clerical adults, when they were befriended, expressed doubt as to whether it was entirely proper for Dominicans and Franciscans to be housed in the same dormitory.

It was the singing, more than what was sung, that bothered me most. I couldn't imagine why they allowed the boys to sing so badly. Or was it perhaps the kind of racket they aimed at? In an attempt to find out, I made various requests to attend rehearsals. These were invariably answered in a gracious affirmative: a small enough favor, for there would be no rehearsals until Christmas time, or until the Holy Year was upon them. Sadly, the situation was partially due to financial circumstances, the inability to give the kids a stipend—and Carlo Rossini declared in disgust: "No mon', no praisa da Lord!" A little severe, for any kind of recompense was hard to come by, and who could gauge what had emerged from meager help in this matter, from the orphan choir school of Gregory the Great to the song-pence granted Palestrina, Haydn, Mozart, Schubert, or Janáček? Father Laurence Feininger, working in the library at St. John Lateran, observed that funds seemed to be available for random works of masonry, which he deemed of no greater importance.

The singing tradition of clerics was something else. I noted that on All Souls' Day in St. Peter's the celebrant sang the Preface as if he were tripping through a cold rain astride a battery-charged mule; that the canons, sitting in their choirstalls in various degrees of ermine, rambled through the Little Hours in much the same haphazard way as our diocesan clergy at priests' funerals, except that they sang as they rambled, and that could only make matters worse: a prolonged, purgatorial sort of cant. So that maybe Carlo was right when he said recently that the offices were only sung on Sundays anymore, because the Vatican feared that the singing was inviting atom bombs to drop on the basilicas.

There was, to be sure, decent enough chant each Sunday at San Anselmo, albeit as nearly porcelainlike as that of the Abbey of Solesmes. Not of the hybrid strength of an international house, and unnecessarily accompanied by a thuddy organ and an organist of thuddy persuasion who had to imagine that chant couldn't go it alone. But in the Sistine Chapel, at the annual Mass for the deceased cardinals, there was a measure of what might have been. At the Absolution, the celebrant sang uncommonly well. He was Pius XII, and maybe that phantasy called "Bach and the Heavenly Choirs"—all about the fiddler Pontiff who vainly battled the Curia to canonize Johann Sebastian—had something going for it. In the wonted tiny gallery, Perosi led the Sistine Choir through a notable reading of his unpublished *Requiem,* and there were only a few of the hardly avoidable foibles of the choirloft: the nervous tapping of the baton before the song, like the whirring of a clock before it strikes.

What Pius XII called "religious music," on the other hand, flourished in the concert halls. At the Umbrian Festival that fall, I heard, in the Cathedral of Assisi, three world premieres: Salviaci's *Il pianto della Madonna,* Liviabella's *Caterina di Siena,* and Clausetti's *San Giovanni Laterano* (possibly forgotten by now, they were a lot more venturesome than the going Church-bound Perosis and Refices); and the Italian premiere of the Poulenc *Mass in G.*

Bonaventura Somma, Magister Choralis at the state Academy of St. Cecilia, held forth admirably at the Teatro Argentina. One doesn't imagine that Vaughan-Williams was much known in Roman ecclesiastical circles at that time, but Somma was performing his *Civitas Sancta.* And I shall never forget his delivery of the Monteverdi *Beatus Vir.* Twenty-six years later, I was electrified at hearing it again during a New Oxford Choir rehearsal to which, I must confess to David Lumson, I hadn't been paying all that much attention. I hadn't known that it was ever published, though I had pestered Somma for it right up until the time he died. His performance had been billed as the first in Rome (of the *realizzazione di Grazzi*) and I assumed that it would join his other De Santis editions of Monteverdi, Scarlatti, Pasquini, Pergolesi, and Animuccia.

I never heard Somma blunder. When his Santa Cecilia Chorus later toured the United States for Sol Hurok, I vaguely remember one or the other diffident review in the New York papers, but of course he couldn't travel with the resources available at the Argentina. When the choir arrived at Boys Town on a Saturday afternoon, Father Wegner had stocked the choir room with wine, and I looked forward to a pleasant weekend. But there was more turmoil in that room than at a six o'clock intersection in Rome. Somma, in the manner of those impeccable but gesticulating traffic directors, finally got through to me: it was Saturday, and the men especially wanted to be paid. Our Boys Town Choir check was no good, and He needed $4,000 in cash in small denominations. A particularly resourceful counselor in my employ got it from a bookie within the hour.

The last time I saw Somma, the Santa Cecilia Choir was performing the Pizzetti *Requiem* under the direction of the composer in the new aula on the Via della Consolazione. I looked and looked—until I noticed a much too vigorous hand movement in the upper righthand flank of the chorus. It was Somma, singing lustily and doing a little surreptitious conducting on the side. We had lunch in a Roman fishery the next day, and he pointed proudly to a sleek, large, and beautiful specimen scarcely out of the water. Its glassy, upturned eye looked suspiciously like his own when he meant business.

I don't think that I ever told him that we had at Boys Town what Moe Szynskie gave the official name of the "Somma Choir." I am not sure that he would have been altogether pleased, for it was the beginners' group. His own compositions were usually, not always, infectious, lilting affairs of the quality of a well-thought-out vocalise. They sang themselves, and the kids took to them instantly. He could have done a lot for the bogged-down singing Church. But a friend of mine once told me that the sorrow of his life was that he had not ever managed to attain a position in the Sistine Chapel. I should like to think he was not passed by, as Palestrina was once dismissed, because he was not a cleric. He was well along, nearly dead, before Bertolucci was appointed. The simple fact is that Perosi lived too long, for the Maestro di Cappella Sistina is a lifetime job, like that of the popes, and Perosi outlasted four of them, even though during a period of nervous prostration he once notified the Roman press that he had become a Methodist.

The Mid-Seventies

It was a different kind of rubble in 1975, more universal, less promising, more depressing. But exercising a quite careful selectivity, one found some things worthy of emulation, a few moments of pride. In the United States, there were two visits to seminaries of high tradition. If the first seemed a shambles, the second posited hope. On St. Joseph's Day, the only persons in the chapel in clerical garb were the concelebrants. Acolytes, lectors, and the rest appeared to be AIM activists or men holding themselves in readiness for the World Tennis Tour. Karsh of Ottawa would have found no subjects for his "Praying Hands." The only music worth mentioning was the Lutheran Agnus, "Christ, O Lamb of God."

The professor of music didn't know what most of the rest was. A good deal of mimeographed material had been left there by departing guests, he said. It was part of the newly structured school of pastoral ministry to let the students plan the music, and it wasn't entirely plain to me why they kept a man of his knowledge and experience around.

The Sanctus opened with a Hosanna that turned out to be a response to every other line of text, cued in usually by an organ glissando. I was introduced to the custom, seemingly universal, of accompanying everything, from the cantor's solo in the responsorial psalms to the chants of the celebrant. Even if there is some show of reason for not placing much faith in a cantor, why underline his debility? I had assumed that, no matter what the position of the altar, the celebrant still addressed the Canon to the Deity. He seemed here to address the congregation, with all the histrionic flair of a graduate of the Curry School of Expression. Concelebrants and readers alike had passed the Liturgical Conference's lector-Rorschach tests with flying colors, right down to the appointed smiles. Not so great an Amen closed the Canon with unheard-of aplomb. Someone started to harmonize, then changed his mind. The congregation rocked in a spasm of laughter, and someone tittered: "We need a choir!" The custom of receiving Communion in the hand is by now almost universally optional, and there is not much sense in the American bishops' making an issue of it if their provincial seminaries do not.

St. Benedict's Day was a great contrast, even though there was no traditional music, unless one were to so codify the Widor *Toccata*. Items reminiscent of chant were the Englished Pater and the Per Ipsum, which is the one thing that concelebrants all over the world seem to belt out in identical fashion. Inevitably it ends dropping a minor third, and the response never ascends to the second in preparation for the chant of the Our Father. In this hallowed place, there had been an early notion that everything must be manufactured anew. Some of the manufacturing was not bad, some of it was amateurish. I thought only one solo, of a kind of Hollywood-Moorish vintage, downright jejune. The quality of the schola, cantor, and congregational response, the integration of all elements, was model. The quondam chant professor, who no longer likes some of his own manufacturing, thinks that Gregorian will come back. The music majors are asking for it, and there is a plainsong Latin Ordinary once a week.

In a neighboring metropolitan cathedral, the *esprit de corps* and performance of a large mixed choir was quite as good as ever. Its repertoire ran through chant, polyphony, and the Viennese classics. It is supported by clergy and congregation alike, being held to English only when the bishop puts in an appearance. Someone who thought the *Victimae Paschali* was a remnant of the old Good Friday liturgy objected to its revival on the ground that Pope John had banished the "perfidious Jew" phrase once and for all. There is a large contingent of young folk in the choir. That, rather than experimental liturgies which never seemed to finish experimenting in Newman Centers, seemed to be the "in" thing among neighboring university students.

New York Holy Week

There were numerous listings of special Holy Week music in the Saturday *New York Times,* but the lead article ran: "Church Music Low-Keyed." Reduced budgets had led some to rely on wandering minstrels. Holy Family Church on East Fourth Street serves the United Nations Community. The Palm Sunday High Mass had deacon, subdeacon, and three lay lectors for the Passion. The professional choir was superb in Casciolini, Pergolesi, and Croce. The Our Father was harmonized and sung by the choir, but at least it was not the Malotte, brandished by a particularly melodramatic pastor in Milwaukee. Some would rail at what might be imagined a breakdown in participation. In that community, however, response and hymn might possibly have been enhanced by the use of Latin. I was edified by the proportion of men and young people. And for the first time the handshaking seemed to me to make some sense, although it was done all over again afterward outside the Church.

The crowd at St. Peter's LCA Lutheran for Jazz Vespers that afternoon was not large or young, but it was congenial. And it was meditative, for the music, interspersed by scriptural texts in a somewhat loose Vesper form, was meant to be a vehicle of meditation. The performers, from the composing mallet-girl at the amplified xylophone, down through trumpet, traps, and bass viol, were expert indeed. I kept thinking that this Lutheran ministry to the jazz community in the dark, slightly forbidding Gothic of Central Presbyterian, for all that it was well appointed, would probably not have been relished by Woodrow Wilson.

One of the several glorious things about the Bach *St. John Passion* at the Episcopal Church of St. Thomas that night was that no one, not even the soloists, used—or needed—any amplification. The boys, I thought, were better than they were twenty-five years ago, when a successor to Tertius Noble is supposed to have said, "If it's a bigger sound they want, I'll give it to them." Pitch, timbre, balance, technique, and interpretive power were mostly exquisite, except for the countertenor, who had all the shrill accuracy and color of an orchestral train whistle. Gere Hancock's wife was at the organ, but I wondered whether the countertenor had been impaneled to make it an all-male production. (I wondered, too, how that little black kid got in there!) A particular cult of "performance practice" is an especial gripe of Paul Henry Lang. It's absurd, he says, to do what Bach had to do in Leipzig just because St. Thomas was short of funds: manage with less than minimal forces. In Belgium, I would run into buffs who reconstructed period organs —of the time of Couperin, say—that way, even if authenticity demanded that the pipes be made of mud.

The downtown churches on Holy Thursday and Good Friday were packed, albeit not as in the old days, when the police had to cordon off Thirty-first Street. The congregations were largely elderly folk, and the liturgist told one of them, "The choir is here only to lead you." It followed the lead pretty well in some traditional hymns, a little in an outdated three-by-three chant

Kyrie, but was nonplussed about where to follow in a decent enough Lemacher Gloria. The traffic in St. Patrick's resembled Grand Central Station fifty years before Amtrak. The chorus was ultraprofessional and bellicose, singing none of the traditional Good Friday liturgy or its texts. But the precentor was possibly the finest I have come across, and he managed to elicit some response to the reasonably well-set, if not well-patterned, psalmic declamations by the simple expedient of raising high his arms. The sermon had something to do with master art pieces of the crucifixion and *Godspell*. The preacher thought that the final shouts of "Long Live God!" were peculiarly pertinent. That wasn't the way I had heard that well-rocked, animated cartoon of St. Matthew at the Off Broadway Promenade the day before. Done with sparkling professionalism, there was more reverence than blasphemy about it, a popular Sabatier sort of expression. But when the Christ said, "I am dead," they hauled him out through the audience, and that was the end of it. Unless one was supposed to read the Resurrection into the curtain calls.[3]

I arrived at St. Clement's Episcopal Church in time for the seventh station of the "Contemporary Stations—an Experiment in Liturgy and Theatre." It turned out to be our eleventh, and I thought perhaps I had misunderstood "eleven" for "seven," much as I had once gone to a poker party which turned out to be a polka party. But not so, the eighth was the twelfth. The fire department allowed only ninety-four attendants, but all ninety-four were there. A cassocked man read the scriptural texts. There were two lighted candles alongside the offering basket, and six on the stage, as if surrounding a catafalque. During the seventh station, a girl played a plaintive flute solo, and played it well. NBC-TV was there for that, and caused a good deal of commotion. At the eighth (twelfth) station, the six candles were moved back, and six grey-robed ballerinas danced to a tinny reproduction of the Verdi *Dies Irae*. They cavorted well enough, but I don't know why.

Easter was, unhappily, something of a musical bust. To get off the beaten path, I traveled up to Ninth and Amsterdam, where a Catholic Church had advertised Anton Heiller's *English Mass*. That was at 10:00 A.M. It was not Heiller, but one of the poorer

exemplifications of the four-hymn syndrome. The 11:00 A.M.
and the 1:00 P.M., in Spanish and French, were more of the
same. Nobody rehearsed with the priest, who was rehearsing a
Spanish hymn before the 11 o'clock service; but it was good to
see the place fill with Latins and blacks, young and old: relaxed,
simpatico, and a thousand different kinds of Signs of the Cross.
Once again, the handshaking seemed in place, and I felt honored to be on the receiving end. On the subway going up, the
lone Caucasian in the car had moved up to where I was sitting,
and someone said: "Father, I think Whitey is afraid."

The best pickings of the great week were at Episcopalian
churches. On Palm Sunday, there had been Evensong and Benediction at St. Mary the Virgin, with the Passion of Resinarius.
I thought it noteworthy that they could attract volunteer profes-
sionals for these evening services. There weren't many people
there—not enough to titillate show-offs or induce climbers. But
I heard the *Vexilla Regis* again, and a proper Palm Sunday improvisation on it at the end, under the customary cloud cover
of incense.

The church was nearly filled for Tenebrae on Wednesday
night, the large and attentive crowd emitting scarcely a cough
throughout the long, sometimes exquisite declamations of the
King James Psalter. The fifteen or twenty clerics in the sanctuary
supplied only the lessons, and I supposed the whole to be the
Burgess English setting.[4] In working out a kind of conglomerate
vernacular Tenebrae, I had once considered some of his chants
and lamentations in need of revision, but I regret not having
kept his psalmody. The responses were Victoria, Ingegneri,
Anerio, and Palestrina, filling and then lingering about the
vaulted spaces of the edifice. No ecclesiastical cop was needed
to tell the congregation when to stand, kneel, sit, or genuflect.
At the end, only the city light filtered through the high un-
shaded windows back of the altar, and we walked out of the
darkness to be greeted by a Holy Week drunk, solo-barking the
Hallelujah Chorus of the *Messiah.*

The Holy Thursday Solemn Eucharist at St. Ignatius was like
something one remembered. A devout immersion in the *Book of
Common Prayer,* and every minute detail of the old Roman ritual.
Only the readings, prayers, and responses were in English. How

could one be so lucky on that day as to hear something as appropriate as the Josquin *Missa Pange Lingua* and all of the Gregorian Propers beautifully done? Prayerful singing. There were only eight well-integrated voices, the women under more perfect polyphonic control than elsewhere. The choirmaster told me later that he had been to Solesmes twice, and that he conducted according to the ictic markings, but transcribed into modern notation for the choir so as to cover the music quickly. I wouldn't have known it, for I thought he had simply stressed the inherent rhythm of the neumes, and I assured him that it was better chant than I expected to hear at Solesmes. He was already using the new *Graduale Romanum* with the several changes proper to the restored Roman rite.

There were the solo verses of the Gradual with choral repeats and occasional antiphonal variations. The congregation joined in singing *Credo I* and the *Pange Lingua,* the choir harmonizing alternate verses so cleanly that I fancied the organ was still accompanying. That, and the haunting Duruflé *Ubi Caritas,* as they neared the repository. It was splendid. And it was sad. I counted a congregation of about forty men and six women. I have heard smart enough remarks about the Anglican liturgy's not having worked from people who were loath to blame any part of the now diminished congregations of the Roman Church on *its* liturgy. If anything is clear, it's that the vernacular didn't save it. I hoped that a working day in near midtown Manhattan might offer a partial explanation.

At the Riverside Church on Easter Sunday afternoon one couldn't quarrel with Frederick Swan's elegant dispatch of the Sowerby *Passacaglia* or his judicious accompaniment of a fine soloist in the Weinberger *Emmaus Solo-Cantata,* though the piece struck me as a kind of Malotte Avenue through the Holy City.

The musical Evensong at St. Bartholomew was a fitting and triumphant enough climax to the Easter parade, slightly redolent of the Waldorf across the street. Choir and soloists in what the rector called the Dvorak *"tedeum"* were first-rate; but there was no way that they, or even the brass choir or the congregation, could score on the vast and tubby organ. Before its manipulator had thoroughly murdered the Widor *Toccata* yet again, I repaired to St. John's, where Father Walter was just finishing the 5:15 P.M. low Mass. He had also taken the 11:00 A.M. and the office chores in between. I went into the empty church to say my Vespers, the while a graying black woman gently told each Station of the Cross aloud to her toddling grandchild. It was the better part of Easter, 1975.

Conference

The Valparaiso University Choir, of excellent balance and texture, enhanced, along with Paul Manz's expert hymn playing, a Lutheran Conference of Church Musicians in Rochester, New York. They sang a plainchant Vesper service and a Latin Mass Ordinary of Weinhorst, which distressed me only because I had somehow missed making its acquaintance previously. A Church Music Editors' Conference at the Westminster Choir College, Princeton, New Jersey, and a Yale Church Music Institute regalement of mostly Union Theological alumni, entitled "New Dimensions in Music and Worship," provided some good music but few new dimensions.[5]

The editors at Westminster were not free-lance folk but music publishers' editors. A place with the muscle of Westminster should have been telling *them* what to do. But subsequent summer workshops that I looked in on were usually subsidized by publishers, and too often only their own music was performed. No one knew where Church music would go in the next ten years, because no one knew where the liturgy was going. At both places, undergrads were rightly concerned about landing jobs, and one headmaster said that that was a far better situation than held in the 60s, when many didn't give a damn whether they got a job or not. The New Oxford Choir was a notable addition to the Yale event, but David Lumson hadn't all that much to do with planning an especially eclectic service with an especially *Godspell*-like *Pax*. I came near to being stuck with a large half-empty chalice that was being passed around. But the alumni at Yale and the gathered gentry at Princeton participated well indeed. It might have been more helpful to have observed an actual lab session of the student planners. As it was, we were told to wait for the new liturgy to impregnate a culture. What liturgy and what culture were different matters.

Finally, on the American side, there was a new kind of sung

Mass at the cathedral in Baltimore. A good one, once you ac-
climated yourself to a kind of defiance of any "High Mass"
tradition. Of the Ordinary, only the Sanctus was sung, and of
the celebrant's chants and their responses, only the "Through
him, With him." The boys and men of the choir were first-rate,
overridden a little too often by organ and amplified cantor. The
largest musical portions were the Offertory and Communion
meditations, Gospel narratives as I recall—something the
hymn-makers at Westminster had warned us against. They were
good, they were contemporary, and they were long. It was not
a children's Mass, but the celebrant insisted on obviating the
intent of the Canon, often using the proper *Jesus* instead of its
pronoun. A choirboy told me that all but one of their number
were from the parish.

Toronto and Montreal

The two most inspiring adventures in this hemisphere, or anywhere, were Canadian. No one could better service a church,
and by extension a whole neighborhood, than the devoted team
who manage St. Michael's Choir School in Toronto. They over-
see four remarkably good sung Masses in the cathedral, three
on Sunday and one Saturday evening, and on Sunday evening
a graduate handles a folk Mass with competence and taste. The
congregation is not slighted at any of them; indeed, the Mass
at which only the congregation sings is not the best attended.
The 300 boys are not resident, so the job is not as simple as it
might sound. One comes in by train each day from sixty-five
miles out. They are well-trained treble stuff, (maturing voices
not so well trained) and the Sunday I was there, the Feast of the
Exaltation of the Cross, there were chant, excerpts of Victoria,
Palestrina, Lotti, Asola, Lassus, and Mozart, and organ works of
Franck and Buxtehude.

The music programed for the 11:30 Sunday Mass was the
same as Saturday evening but there were different choirs singing it, so that my only objection was a selfish one. All of that
service demanded some dissipation of talent, a necessary sacrificing of a single group more top-flight than the rest. But one
doesn't quarrel with the fine educational values, the music, and
the warmth that are St. Michael's.

The choir school at St. Joseph Oratory in Montreal is small by comparison, but the 11 o'clock service each Sunday is as worthwhile as anything on the continent. The choir of about eighty is of the sterling stuff of the Ratisbon Domspatzen ("Cathedral sparrows"). The great loft of the Oratory, high atop Mount Royal, deserves such a choir, and so do the the thousands of devotees of Brother André who come there to worship. They will likely hear a polyphonic Kyrie, Gloria, and Agnus, participate in French responses and acclamations, and recite the Pater and Creed. A polyphonic Creed was sung during the distribution of Communion. Bidding prayers and Elevation acclamations were sung. The new Van Beckerath, truly a *grand orgue,* makes a great contribution. (Students in Toronto did some of the playing on a serviceable old tracker that had been part of a gigantic organ at the Philadelphia Centennial Exposition in 1876.) The Oratory Service, with sermon, lasted fifty minutes.

Both Father Armstrong, Toronto, and Father Dupuis, Montreal, promise increased use of Gregorian. The one is Roman-oriented, and better than anything in Rome. The other is rather Franco-German, and as good as anything in France or Germany.

Rome

Trevi Fountain or no, Rome is pleasant to come back to, maybe because whatever door you step out of you are thrown back a thousand years and more, and you imagine that you know something of history. It was another Holy Year, and the air in so large a place as St. Peter's was fetid with pilgrims. The music was no better or worse than it ever had been, and in these days one puts that down as a plus—and another proof that language has nothing to do with musical quality.

The first thing I ran into was quite a dreadful reconciliation mini-Vesper service at St. Peter's. With a printed Latin and Italian order of service in hand, those to be reconciled tried vainly to sing against a witless organ accompaniment and divers processions of pilgrims singing their own thing in Babel. Afterwards, Paul Cardinal Marella, proud only of being eighty, made a gesture of apology. "Aah," he said, in the kind of guttural

Italian that comes close to "ach," "What can you expect in St. Peter's?" I think he would have said it of nearly every church in Rome, though he is more Roman than Italian, and the Romans are more international than any modern one-worlder. I told him how proud I had been to note, during the telecast of the opening of the Holy Year, that he was the only prelate who sang the responses without benefit of book. And I told him that I brought no good news from home. "Aah, sooner or later," he seemed to say, "there is no good news anywhere."

At St. Mary Major, a small group of professional male cantors declaimed *Mass VIII,* with the kind of ersatz polyphonic versettes previously alluded to thrown in. During the chant, canon, nun, and layperson hacked away individually at the tune. But it was good to hear the Proper of the Fifth Sunday after Easter again, the soaring *Vocem Jucunditatis,* even if accompanied. Should I live to be older than Marella, I shall never understand the misuse of the organ. Nor that of the omnipresent microphone. Pius XI, I believe, considered the Marconi invention a great boon to evangelic endeavor, and that is all right. But why in every church and chapel, from Solesmes to the meanest convent of the Poor Clares? I have never attended a liturgy in a two-car garage, but I am sure that someone would discover a "need" for one there, as well.

It was the same thing at St. John Lateran, although there were some boys to brighten the figurated music. Enroute to St. Paul's Outside the Walls, at one or the other parish church, one heard a dim organ backdrop, as in a funeral parlor. Except at St. Suzanna, the American church, where a guitarist had no luck with an impossible congregational Alleluia. The bright spots at Vespers in St. Paul's were a couple of visiting choirs, one as prelude, the other, a brightly togaed contingent of Africans, as participants.

The garbage that infested the usually trim environs of St. Paul's was incredible. It wasn't the fault of the Romans or the Africans, who weren't buying all that much from the food vendors, and who had the decency to wander back to the drains to urinate. Anyway, don't ever let any anxious native of any country try to explain the hour of service, or the hour of a train, in English. Better that you guess what, say *halb fünf* means, lest you spend the night. But the bells got me to Vespers almost on time. There was the sparse, divided choir of monks, the abbot, two black bishops, and four cantors in front of the mike.

On any day, a mike is excusable in St. Paul's, but on that day, pilgrim groups carried portable outfits, and it was mike against mike, amplifying disaster. The chief cantor conducted the gathering by ever so sleight-of-hand—chironomy seems to be out. The organist pitched things so high that whoever was of a mind to sing seldom came within a minor second of the reciting tone, and many relaxed to the octave. I wondered what the Africans up front thought of all these macabre goings on, and I was relieved when, at a benign and somewhat bemused signal from the cantor, they began to sing a truly rousing Alleluia to the accompaniment of their native rhythm instruments, which were a good deal less barnacled than the organ. A TV person stuck yet another mike out over the klieg lights, and a knowing black lady started drifting into western thirds. I thought they might have appreciated the sound of a gong or two at Benediction, as I would have, and that if the monks had to sing Vespers, they might have done so in the privacy of the adjoining monastic choir.

Back at St. Peter's, one was all but crushed in the crowds in the crypt, and it was perhaps symptomatic that not many appeared to be asking questions at the tomb of Pius X, upstairs. Golden shafts of sunlight shot down through Michelangelo's dome like the bolts hurled from on high in the pictures of Saul at Damascus. Maybe, in the midst of all this latter-day brouhaha, they would find another Saul, throw him from his horse, and reconvert us Gentiles.

I missed, that day, the High Mass at San Anselmo, which the abbot primate said had been better than usual. He was still smarting, but not too much, over a letter that had gone from some cranky dowager to all the abbots in the world. It seems that she had certified San Anselmo as the place to go for Midnight Mass. So her traveling friends dutifully went to a rock Mass. The primate is not boss of the house, hadn't arranged it, wasn't aware. Currently the International House sings a Gregorian High Mass with Italian trimmings. For the Office, it divides into different language groups. At the Pontifical Institute there are no services, and Monsignor Ferdinand Haberl,[6] who bears the family name well, must miss Sundays at St. Cecilia's in Regensburg.

San Giorgio in Venice is proud of its sixteenth-century choir-books and Vivaldi manuscripts, and the several remarkable paintings left them after Napoleon raped the place. It is the only church on either side of the canal that advertises a sung Mass *cum cantu Gregoriano.* When Rome said that there must not be two altars in the sanctuary, Abbot Giles removed the temporary one. Above the other is a striking sculpture of the four evangelists holding high God's world. He says Mass, not with his back to the congregation, but to Apollo raising the Venetian maritime world, directly in line across the water.

Belgium
No one in Louvain knew of anything worthwhile there. The times were bad for Church music, they said, and the pride of the country, the St. Rombout Choir of the Metropolitan Cathedral in Malines, had been disbanded. But high above the gigantic brewery and the town, there was still the Abbey of Mont César. Father Vitry would be pleased to know that, though the glory Josef Kreps and he sought to bring it is no longer apparent, it is still a prayerful oasis. The books in the choirstalls ranged from the new Gradual to the 1893 Solesmes Antiphonary. One of the latter, surely not Vitry's, had some rhythmic signs penciled in. He would rejoice that the chant, perhaps a little slow for his liking, is not held up by the *episema.* The full Greogrian Propers are well sung each day in Latin: the Sanctus, Agnus, Pater, and acclamations, in the vernacular, seemed a considerable improvement over the sometimes soggy Flemish office chants of Lauds.

Across town is the venerable Lemmensinstituut which Canon Josef Joris brought here from Malines in the high hope, yet to be realized, of affiliation with the prestigious university. It is an altogether impressive Church music school, large, professional, alert. There are some seventy-five instructors of 150 to 160 students, who stay from one to five years for several kinds of certification: organ, choir, chant, music education, Orff, the dance, art. The spacious old asylum which houses them still has double windows (one inoperable), put there so that attendants might tell worrisome suicidal wards: "Of course you may open the window."

There are two choirs for the chapel liturgy, where major works like the Bach *St. Matthew Passion* are also produced; and there are more possibilities of placement than graduates. In Malines, Flor Peeters still does his turn at the organ, and the children sometimes sing chant, but he's careful not to show up if he thinks the liturgy is going to be out of hand. His wife, Marieka, tolerates terrible music in church as a penitential matter and a sufferance for Flor.

Beuron, West Germany

Although the once flourishing school of liturgical art is gone, the monks still sing a Gregorian High Mass each day, but there was not much *lux et origo* about *Ordinary I* the day I heard them. The Graduales and Antiphonaries are of 1920 vintage, for there is certainly a pertinent question of being out of pocket every time a new book comes out. Anyway, the Latin is a problem for the ninety lay brothers who comprise two-thirds of the abbey's personnel. They use a German Psalter got out by a monk from Erscheinen. It is in Gregorian notation, but no kind of direct adaptation. My very gracious guide was Oxford-trained in Sanskrit. The liturgical movement, he thought, had become too noisy and unmeditative. At Beuron, he is busy the year around giving Zen retreats.

Luxembourg

The proliferation of languages in Luxembourg makes a vernacular liturgy there difficult. I missed the High Mass, Vespers, and the rosary at Sacré Coeur. At the Cathedral of Notre Dame, there was a quiet Italian Mass—but no Italian sermon—in the crypt. Upstairs the celebrant started singing a Communion song, and the people sang well enough until he found the mike and submerged them. He hadn't waited for the organist, who had to play catch-up, but who got even in the end with a kind of noisy transcription of Napoleon's Last Charge.

The later Radio High Mass was therefore a pleasant surprise: a large, good-sounding choir in a marvelous acoustical setting.

Ordinary and Proper alike were French and a bit flamboyant, the Alleluia and Verse, a "Frère Jacques" folk chorale sung antiphonally with an excellent clerk-cantor.

That afternoon, in the village of Sandsweiller, the St. Cecilia Choir celebrated its 125th anniversary. It sang a *Canticle of St. Cecilia* written for the occasion by Jean-Pierre Schmit in Letzemberger. There was an excellent baritone in selections from Gershwin and Kern, and six bands in the parade. It didn't look to me as if the villages were losing their identity, as Jean-Pierre said they were. On the way back to the city, past Radio Free Europe, he regaled me with stories about the second bishop of Luxembourg, Koppes by name and a presumed relative of my mother. He was a hardy old gentleman who could bend a coin in his hand. He wasn't buried in the cathedral because he had raised too much hell with the Masons. And when, near the end of his life, he suffered disorders of the urinary tract, he told his worried relatives: "So you see I am no longer the episcopus of Luxembourg—only the piscopus."

Cologne

Churches in Cologne, the "Rome of the North," were well supplied with prayer and song books put out by the German conference of bishops. They contained the Mass, Latin chants with German underlay, German chants in Gregorian nomenclature, and hymns. Some said that the book tried to do too much, that it was not as successful as a 1970 edition, that one or the other diocese had already abandoned it, and that—as seems to have happened every place else in the world—topflight musicians who hung in with the commissions until the bitter end had been able to give them little enough direction.

At St. Peter's, a traveling madrigal choir from Munich was to sing the following Sunday. The posted schedules at the cathedral were as impressive as ever, and its choir better than I remembered it in an Ordinary by Neckes and Gregorian Propers that danced. There was a great profusion of flowers and May altars everywhere, and I thought of Jaroslav Pelikan's excellent lecture on *Lex orandi, Lex credendi* at Colgate in Rochester. He had agreed that precipitate and radical change in *orandi* had to affect *credendi,* wondered how many Catholics gave passing thought to May being upon us, and told the assemblage that, while Mary didn't come through in the Augsburg Confession, they might think twice when they sang the second verse of "Ye Watchers and Ye Holy Ones":

> *O higher than the cherubim*
> *More glorious than the seraphim . . .*
> *Alleluia*
> *Thou bearer of th' Eternal Word*
> *Most gracious, magnify the Lord*
> *Alleluia*

Michael Schneider, on the *Evangelisch* side, said that Johann Nepomuk David was over and done with, that Stockhausen and tapes were in, and that the two percent cut in the German Church tax hadn't helped matters. (English choir schools too were fighting budgetary problems and a bias about preferential treatment.) Stockhausen may have reverted to simple Grecian melodies, but the mimed drama of his *Herbst-Musik* was a good forty-five minutes longer than Florentine patience last spring. A critic reported cryptically that in Part I the composer and a colleague drive nails into the plank of a roof; in Part II, he and three others break some twigs; and in Part III, flail some wheat. In the Finale, a prepuberty love scene, a boy and a girl roll in some dry leaves, wet themselves in the rain, then play a viola and clarinet duet. The Florentines had probably not taken kindly to the composer's suggestion of a prior four-day fast to heighten their awareness either. Should he really get back to writing children's music, he will perhaps ask them to lay off candy during Lent.

Paris

In Paris, Jean Langlais said that the Holy Ghost was on strike. He was talking about the Church and its music, not the noisy Germans whose spring invasion of the place came close to matching that of 1940. At St. Francis Xavier, they have a sung Latin Mass at 9:00 and one in French at 11:00. But Gaston Litaize, the staff organist, hasn't all that much to do, for they play Beethoven records betwixt and between. At Notre Dame, the Little Singers were peddling their records among the great crowds of tourists, and it was difficult to hear, above the din, a good-sounding English chorus and orchestra in concert. The audience strained to see the countertenor—like a freak on display. The Southwark people were to sing for three of the Sunday Masses, but I did not see much of Pentecost in the scheduled song. The Lindburgh boys were to be there Monday, and Marilyn Mason on the morrow. One must arrive a half hour ahead of time for the weekly organ recitals.

The Sunday Masses at St. Clotilde were varied, with cantors at the ambo conducting nothing in particular—a little like Father Missia conducting himself when he sang. Jean Langlais opened the 11:00 with the first Franck *Chorale.* The organ is rich, mighty, gutty, and great beyond desire. Two stones at the entry commemorate Franck, who had forty registers, and Tournemire, who added twenty. Jean asked for only two. (Flor Peeters had told me how several noted organists, examining Franck's original console in the Peeters studio, were astounded at the listing of reed mixtures, and how Tinel had confessed to his orchestra quite late in life: "Gentlemen, I, Tinel, was wrong. Cesar Franck is a great composer.") Just before Mass, I was startled by the organ prelude theme, briefly amused, then deeply moved. It was a short and beautiful improvisation, more threnody than whimsy, on "When Morning Gilds the Skies," which Jean had often heard Moe's chancel choir sing as a processional at Boys Town. Only I, in St. Clotilde, was aware of the gesture.

There was a part of Jean's unpublished *Songs of Brittany* at the Offertory, utterly unobtrusive, meditative playing through the Canon, and the first part of his *Apocalypse* (which he said he had read forty times during his recent illness) at Communion. From the first gallery, a physician friend led a volunteer choir through *Mass VIII* and part of the *Veni Creator.* Jean said that, if the curé had been home—but never on Pentecost or Christmas—it would have been Gelineau or worse. The congregational Alleluia was the now universal, old Holy Saturday one. It is no longer something to be waited for, symbolic as the first clap of thunder after winter. But Pentecost was a powerful improvisation on the *Veni Creator,* and an extended one after Mass on the *Te Deum.* I remembered how an old teacher, speaking of Marcel

Dupré at St. Sulpice, had often fancied that the greatest music was never written down.

The bland humor of the blind has always amazed me: Paul Doyon of Montreal, "looking" at our campus, happy at the "sight" of the first snow. I once asked Langlais how long it took him to walk from his sixth-floor apartment to St. Clotilde, and he said, "Fifteen minutes alone, twenty with my wife." This time, as Marie-Louise Jaquet, titular organist at Mulhouse,[7] drove us through a brightly lighted Saturday night on the inevitable tour of the city, Jean described the new skyscrapers, and regaled us with the story about the Texan who kept pestering his guide about how long it had taken to build structures like Notre Dame. "A thousand years? . . . We would do it in six months!" The next day he asked how long that new and towering office had been a-building, and the guide said: "I wouldn't know—it wasn't there yesterday."

(There are all those stories which peers tell about the redoubtable Maurice Duruflé, who in the quondam French manner, still considers anything beyond the border barbarous. If a German piece begins with "b" he will write down "by Brahms." Serving on a jury with Flor Peeters, he remarked: "My goodness, you speak French, Flemish, German, English—and play the organ besides!" When he noted that he didn't like a piece, and Flor said, "But, Maurice, you must give a reason," he replied: "All right. I don't like it *at all!*")

And someplace in Paris, in an arena I believe, there was said to be a weekly gathering of some 4,000 who insisted on singing chant at a Latin Mass. The phenomenon has officially disappeared under cloud of the heresy of Trent.

Solesmes

Friends ask me (a) how come they let me in, and (b) how come they let me out? I was so totally impressed that I did indeed toy with the idea of staying, as Langlais had predicted I might. It wasn't the laundered but rough and unpressed sheets that deterred me. It was so cold that I feared I might spend most of the time in bed to keep warm. I wondered, too, through the never-ending offices of night and day, about losing the mundane satisfaction of reflecting that I had "finished" my prayers.

I paid my respects at the graves of all the patriarchs except Josef Pothier, who I guess is still at St. Wandrille. At that of Dom Gajard, I thought of him there in the garden telling Langlais: "Hear the blackbird! It doesn't know what an *ictus* is, yet it sings better than we." I was supplied with a monastic breviary, a 1936 Antiphonary, and a new Graduale. Compline reminded me of Tenebrae at St. Mary's in New York. Vesper incense hadn't entirely lifted, and one couldn't follow texts in the dark.

The abbey couldn't be faulted for the crowd of onlookers, all breathlessly attentive save for the American lady who clopped out in the middle of things. It's a showpiece only because it represents something first-class, and eventually people catch on —like the two German seminarians from Paderborn, a daughter diocese of nearby Le Mons, who, I thought, were to be complimented on their choice for a weekend; or my Shintoist Japanese companion who insisted on standing for the cab fare from Sables, and who, on no provocation at all, bowed deeper than the monks at any rubric.

There is no dearth of vocations to the rigid monastic life at Solesmes, where Prime, Tierce, Sext, and None[8] are still sung in choir—and sung to perfection without organ, except at Compline when at day's end, it might be felt that a crutch is deserved, even if not needed. I agreed with Monsignor Haberl, who had said that, for all the Solesmes books, the old and quite romantic Solesmes Praxis was no longer in vogue.

At Mass, only the readings and bidding prayers were in French, so the Gospel was not sung, but the Latin Canon was. There were no versicle soloists, but there was an expert, unconducted, semicircular schola at the ambo. I had trouble, on this second day of Pentecost, following the Mass chants until about Communion time, when I remembered that the feast no longer rates an octave, and discovered that we were celebrating the Benedictine feast of St. Yvonne, *sacerdos.* I am only mildly and occasionally disturbed by the displacements of the new Roman calendar, but I find that it is one of the chief thorns for some. France is way ahead of us on holidays that cut down the work week, and I could not make a connection back to Chartres. So I made a desultory survey of the mimeographed French hymns scattered around churches in Sables and Le Mons, and bought some strawberry tarts at the corner grocery to assuage the disappointment of rail schedules.

Vienna

An excursion through Vienna on Ascension Thursday mostly bore out a dismal prediction. A church near the station was crowded for First Communion, and a congregational bout with an impossible German Gloria was vain. At eight o'clock, there was the barest scattering of people in the Votivkirche and scarcely audible singing. The small organ up front, a popular "solution" to participation problems, was of no great help to either hymn or truncated Gloria. The good lady who sent me to the Academy Church of St. Ursula, though, was on target. The volunteer student choir chanted exquisitely. It was *all* chant. *Missa Lux et Origo* and the complete, glorious Ascension Gregorian. One knew what day it was. The chant was interspersed with finely wrought and well-chosen organ versettes, like the de Grigny *Veni Creator.* The congregation sang *Credo I* and the Latin responses well. These seem never to pose a problem where, as in the Cologne cathedral, here, and at Aachen, they are still employed. The plaque displaying the names of the *Ehrwürdigen* of the Academy included Walton, Furtwängler, Anglès, Goller, Hindemith. The noon High Mass at St. Stephan's Cathedral was packed. Formidable forces filled the place with the great chant Proper and the Beethoven *Mass in C.* And the organist's thundering improvisation on *Viri Galilaei* was a fitting close to the day.

Canticum Mundi, a book of people's chants edited by Joseph Kronsteiner, which one finds in the pews of Austrian churches, both antedates and outshines the Vatican's *Jubilate Deo.* Despite professional aversion to chant adaptations in the vernacular, these were evident in most of the German and Flemish service books I saw. Europe seems to have been spared the missalette disease, and Canada's English version is modest by comparison to ours. The churches in Vienna were plastered with posters advertising everything from films and seminars on family planning to *Godspell.* In Switzerland Monika Henking carries on a successful ecumenical experiment with a children's choir of some 135, ages nine to sixteen. Anton Heiller wrote his *Advent und Passion-Musik* for them. The taste of the troupe and the temper of their times are reflected in some of their own compositions, which are taped and then transcribed by their mentors.

I remarked to my friend that the Viennese seemed to have retained their *gemütlichkeit.* "Yes," he said, "but when they are disagreeable, they can be very disagreeable." Vainly trying to hail our waiter, he added, "Take that guy, for example. When I was still drinking beer, I always ordered four right off, to be sure I would get them!"

Regensburg

The Regensburg Domspatzen had flown south to concertize, but the old Bavarian town was brim full of music during the centennial week of the *Kirchen-Musikschule.* The commemorative booklet of Masses and concerts was most impressive, and generally the former outshone the latter, and that was proper enough. Norbert Schmid was still doing the exemplary choral work I had heard a dozen years ago. The student voices were woven into a fine fabric, tuned perfectly, with clear and steady treble lines and superb technique. The Hindemith Ordinary and Isaac Propers gave them no trouble at all. His own German High Mass, not especially demanding or contemporary, was nonetheless strong; it moved and brought out the best in the congregation. Whatever formularies were used for the responses must have been well established, for the people thundered them out. The Canon was sung, and the Preface seemed an exact adaptation of the Gregorian, the Pater nearly so. A separate chorale sings the chant out of the new Graduale with inimitable expertise. And it suddenly struck me that I hadn't had my hand shaken, nor heard a fouled-up great Amen since Rome.

One scarcely remembers the time when people crossed over to oriental rites so that they could celebrate in the vernacular. Listening in on the Byzantine Vespers at St. Cecilia's, I wondered that there had been any musical attraction at all. There is the lure of the ceremonies, of course: solemn and exact movements and posture, multiple crossings, and censer-swinging down the aisle. But the harmonized formularies of the male choir, the Waring humming through the celebrant's chants, the cascading textual rushes between solemnities, left me with the decision of saying my own Vespers or telling my beads.

There are around eighty full-time students in the venerable old school, some from as far away as Korea, none at this moment from the United States or Canada, though the 100-year listings in the Jubilee Book give evidence of influence there, as well. Not many clerics anymore; some nuns, and a large preponderance of laymen and laywomen, usually about equally divided. All of this tradition of music-making for the Lord has brushed off onto other city churches. All day Sunday the bells call you to one or the other sung service.

An evening Mass in the Nieder-Münster church was jammed —with a generous portion of youths, some with their dates. It was a cross between the old High Mass and the old *Sing-Messe.* A celebrant of extraordinary voice was a genuine leader of song, never battling the full-throated congregation with a mike. At the Alt-Kapelle, they were having Benediction. A prelate led the rosary from the pulpit, and a small but good women's choir sang an opening Latin hymn for Exposition. There is a sign in the Alt-Kapelle telling how, when the Reformation came to Regensburg in 1542, the Alt-Kapelle held true. I don't know what the Reformation has going for it there now. The Protestant Neupfarr-Kirche was worshiping in a different church downtown which displayed a large poster advertising "Jazz for Jesus."

That night, in the cavernous Minoritenkirche, now only a concert hall, the festivities closed with the Bruckner *Te Deum.* It was an exciting, if something less than monumental, performance, and Norbert Schmid worked hard and effectively to pull it off. The happy, congenial crowd which spilled out of the sparse exits afterward—fire regulations must not exist in Regensburg—had every reason to congratulate itself. One wishes that they might have been singing Bruckner a hundred years ago. They were not. But then, what might have been the impact of the music of the Roman Church if a hundred, or a dozen, provincial towns had attacked the problem as Regensburg had?

Munich
Munich was reported to be liturgically and theologically wild, but except for the great new mall in the center of the city, it might have been any Trinity Sunday of the last several centu-

ries. There was precious little business outside the depot, and the queues at the cinema were not long. Not even the merry-go-round in the clockwork of the City Hall tower seemed to be working by noon, when the mall began to fill with people emptying out of churches. Some liturgists would be nonplussed by the prodigious music schedules posted on most church doors, the May specials and night processions, the plethora of fiddleback chasubles, the spectacle of confessions heard right through Mass. (True from Rome to Montreal.) There was not even comfortable standing room in St. Michael's at the 9:00 A.M. Mass. And no one fidgeted or seemed anxious to get out before every singing cello, every choral climax of the Haydn *Paukenmesse,* had had its say. Not a soul who did not join in the vigorous declamation of the same Gregorian-like, German Our Father, and, as at the Stefansdom in Vienna, the Agnus Dei lasted just through the many Communions, distributed by perhaps five or six clerics. The sermon was long enough for me to catch a part of a Mozart *Brevis,* sounding a little thin in the vastness of the cathedral (Frauenkirche) just up the street.

An elderly nun kept straight my direction to the Theatiner-Kirche. Mass there was a horror to a modern: Eastern position, not a syllable of German, Canon *sotto voce,* and the only instrumentation a quiet organ improvisation on the Communion theme of the day. Even the recessional, for which everyone remained, was choral. The complete and useful Lassus *Missa Qual Donna* was a joy, even though treated to overaccentuation. And so were the chant Propers, complete except for a psalm-tone version of the Gradual verse. Everyone knew the Latin Our Father. And it struck me that the polyphonic settings sanctioned by Trent, which has been romanticized in a puritan sort of way, rendered textual understanding more difficult than the classical settings I had heard a couple of hours earlier. It was a pleasure to hear the solemn Ite again, especially since the celebrant didn't hang on to the first note as if he were afraid to jump.

A kind couple offered to accompany me on the tram to St. George's, which they said was a great distance. But there was no music listed, and I had really just wondered what the Soldaten-und-Kriegerkameraderschaft were up to there. (It was some sort of veteran's gathering, and it wasn't All Souls' Day.) And they said that the Stiftskirche in Weyard was light-years away in the opposite direction from Regensburg—a Kloster—so I missed the 3:00 P.M. *Weisenhaus-Messe* of Mozart. Anyway, it was warmer back on the train, looking out at the village where Katzenjammer kids tagged mischievously after a marching band; spiraeas, giant as trees, were bending in full bloom; and in the forests, fir trees were sprouting fresh green tips like Christmas candles.

England

There was nothing very bright in the British picture. Everyone seemed to think that the Church was in about the same shape the country was—precarious, indeed. No one saw much of a reaction to the sad state of music affairs (the Jazz Mass was not fading, as so many of every religious persuasion elsewhere seemed to think), and they were afraid there wasn't enough faith left to trigger one. Even so, some of the top people had hung in the commissions until the futility of the exercise was plain. The estimable Father Purney still had a choir. Smaller, he said, than the old Westminster Diocesan Choir, but perhaps better. He was preparing for a concert a couple of days hence, and I guessed that it was largely Tudor, with some Palestrina thrown in.

At the Catholic Westminster Cathedral, Collin Mawby still had a choir school of some forty boys to sing daily Mass and Vespers. But there had been considerable uproar about the expense of it, some of it raised by Anthony Milner who, the last time I had him as a guest lecturer at our old Boys Town workshop, was writing a "joyful" complete *Graduale Anglicum* which was never published by Novello-Grey. And lucky for them, no matter how it turned out. I hadn't raised my hand when he asked for a show of approval, and George Carthage had asked: "If you think you are being true to the liturgical moment, do you think you are being true to yourself?" For Milner was a composer of no mean talent. I had carried his finely wrought *St. Matthew Passion Responses* on the road one year, and a Kansas City critic accused us of singing the most gentlemanly *Crucifige* on record. That was not Milner's fault.

I gathered that the grants allowing the choir school's maintenance, and a rather extensive cathedral renovation, were not all of them comprised of "Catholic" money. Anyway, Mawby has been supplied with the new Graduale for the chant, and sings the little English worth singing. One Mass out of eight is Latin, and some of the clergy don't understand why, but they are not long on suggestions for bettering matters. No one I met had ever been opposed to the great liturgical reform. They only felt that it had gone astray.

I traveled across the country, past the sheep herds of the pastoral East, through the cattle herds of the pastoral West, the lovely spring countryside of Bath, and the gently indented valley of the Foss, to spend an afternoon with Dom Gregory Murray at Downside. Long friends, we had never met. I spoke with him once over the phone from London, and when he was in the United States, where shortly before the storm broke he came under some minor episcopal censure for lobbying for the vernacular. He couldn't call on me; he was traveling with Cliff Bennett's GIA troupe, and it wouldn't have been politic. (Dom Gregory, an articulate critic of Solesmes, contributed frequently to *Caecilia,* and Cliff had stolen a march on me.)

He is now the happy shepherd of souls in the nearby village church. From that serene shelf, he views with laughter the pygmy interests that still concern some of us. For all his lifetime of making waves in the sea of this school of chant or that, he considers it to have been a romantic venture. He is not all that happy with ICEL texts and the rest, but deems it not a literary matter. Of all the informed people I have met he seemed the most optimistically buoyant, and he generously excused my reservations, imagining that I lived in quite a different world at Boys Town.

He is still in charge of the monks' music in the handsome abbey church, where the tripart offices are of a Rome-approved English genre of their own. They use his very acceptable pentatonic psalmic arrangements, the cadence of each verse being the reverse of the opening. A Gregorian pattern, I thought. A diminutive Phillips organ, not a transistor and costing about 500 American dollars, gives the monastic choir as much assistance as it might require.

I must confess I had never known those people of the old Church, who he thought reacted largely out of fear and superstition, until the Christian commitment of the new rite of Confirmation came along. But it was good to talk to someone about the old Franciscan notion of the *felix culpa* not having been the *raison d'être* of the Incarnation. And I explained that, whatever my views, I was like the midwesterner of whom it has often been said that you can take the boy out of the country, but not the country out of the boy. For, as I got off the boat at Dover and handed the customs official my passport with my left hand, he genially stuck out his right for my landing card—and I shook it. It wasn't that I had missed a proper *Pax* for some weeks, and surely I didn't imagine that amid the gale that blasted the cliffs that day, nearly blowing a highly touted international golf tournament out to sea, he had been waiting all that time to welcome *me!* But he laughed as if I had thought it all out as a joke, and chided me for not planning to stay longer in Britannia.

Aachen

I had been told that Aachen would be a good place to celebrate Corpus Christi: that the cathedral choir had revived marvelously after several years of quibbling incidental to the death of "Papa" Rehmann. I had the memory of Monsignor Rehmann's kindness at the old choir school, a notable memorial Mass for Pius XII, some of his altogether worthy compositions like the *Missa Cantantibus Organis,* and his pride in his niece-nun in Sioux City, who had written a history of her order in the United States. I heard the full Gradual and verse, and the Alleluia verse, done by a full complement of superb, soaring sopranos. Boys and men alternated during the Sequence *(Lauda Sion),* but sang only four or five verses. That was enough for me because, Thomas Aquinas aside, this late addition to the Gregorian repertoire is no great shakes and nearly as difficult as Webern to sing.

I had forgotten how intimate the liturgy might be in the Byzantine forefront of Charlemagne's old church. Not many canons were there, but outside the richly glassed apse, the place was full. The Mass, composed on a *chanson* by an eighteenth-century choirmaster of the Aachener Dom was economical and expertly done. (There were no strident altos, as one sometimes encounters even in England, and no strident tenors or basses, as one quite often encounters in Germany.) The chant here, too, was sung out of the new *Graduale*, though there were still a few copies of the 1934 Desclée version with German underlay lying around the gallery. The congregation sang its part lustily, mostly in Latin. Outside, in the cathedral square, there were lines of banners and freshly cut young trees for the procession that night. Making my way through the swarms of holiday visitors, I stopped in at St. Marien.

The *Leonardo da Vinci* was not easy to board at Naples, for it was not yet there. Everyone was worried that the fine ship might be permanently tied up alongside the *Raffaelo* in Genoa. One could scarcely fault the Italian government for discontinuing its subsidy for trips like mine, and I thought that some of the generally good-natured ribbing of the affable Italians went a little too far. Like the story of the new Italian tank which had three reverse shifts and one forward, the latter in case of an attack from the rear.

One way and another, during the crossing, two capital companions suggested a trip halfway back to Ireland—to St. John's, Newfoundland, where the music was no better or worse than anywhere else. Where a $100,000 Casavant had been purchased some years before for the basilica's bicentennial. Where a knowledgeable nun now replaces a knowledgeable chap who had been brought over from Regensburg because a knowledgeable bishop considered that a previous director, knowledgeable enough, knew no Gregorian. This last sometimes returns from his duties at the University Extension in Corner Brook to help with the music in my friend's parish in The Goulds. They are a unique and wonderful, sturdy lot, the "Newfies." And I suppose that, for all their kindness, they remarked slyly to their compatriots of me, as they do of anyone from even as close as Halifax or Quebec: "He's from *away.*"

"SING TO US,"
THEY SAID

The Church music scene is no brighter, and hardly any more dismal, than I have pictured it. Composers do indeed feel the chill winds that rustle through the poplars on the shores of exile. And the practitioner who is serious about *music* in the church is indeed tempted by the plaint of Robert Louis Stevenson's vagabond: "I have longed for all, and bid farewell to hope." It has gradually become the fashion to admit the problem. But it is not yet the fashion to pose problems without proposing solutions which only beat the air.

It is not all really that new: Augustine, worrying about whether the churchly chants might be touched more by the first Adam than the second, and all those legalisms to secure for the muse a proper domain; Francis of Assisi, forgoing his lute but striking a tune on two sportive twigs as he walked off into the snowy wood, leaving a trail for all vernacularists and all popular song; Thomas Aquinas, limning theology in verse; people singing and people listening to the songs of the uplands; plainsong and carol, Perotin and Josquin, Haydn and Mozart—and who can say that we have finished or begun?

But it will be at least as long as Heiller suggested before anyone knows whether we have builded or merely smashed; whether we have in fact brought song to the hearts and lips of men; whether, in that evening, we shall come singing like the

psalmist as we bear our sheaves from a vast liturgical harvest—
as Chesterton said that what St. Benedict stored, St. Francis
scattered.

If someone should paint a more lightsome picture a century
from now, it will not have emerged magically from any set of
laws, nor from the frenetic activities of any musical or liturgical
clan, and certainly not from the Tinker Toy projects which beset
us today. Yet one must grant that the human spirit can rise far
above fashion and prejudice. It will happen sometime, some
place, but whether it triggers a trickle or a flood, only history
will record. If it is a trickle, it will be because we have persisted
in raising an antithesis between the popular and the good, and
because we have berated the common intelligence and the common spirit.

It is not just a problem of Church music, or of music going
where the liturgy goes. It is a problem of all music. We can
scarcely be blamed for having settled too much for a strong
tinge of historicity at a time when there were no giants stalking
the land. And there is not much sense in bearing down on hard
rock if the alternative is Lucas Foss: if we abide the invasion of
the crass and materialist science of electronics into the spiritual
domain of melody and rhythm.

So maybe there will be a great liberation one day, but we shall
not see it. Maybe the best of the times will be good and great
again, the heritage of all, because it will surely recognize the
difference between participation and the playing of all parts, the
virtue of a community structured of fitting stones and not just
myriad jigsaw puzzles.

Meanwhile, we might be allowed to face the music with some
small humor, if nothing else. Not all of the dons at the Fifth
International Church Music Congress were amused when Paul
Henry Lang closed out his remarks with the story of "Our
Lady's Juggler." But I fancy it an accurate enough vision:[1] "According to the engaging medieval legend, the Blessed Virgin
accepted the juggler's piety and veneration expressed in somer-
saults before her stone image. Perhaps Mary, in her thousands
of stone images, has watched for centuries with equal tolerance
and sympathy the antics of Church musicians and liturgists; let
us not tempt her patience forever."

APPENDIX:
Caecilia, 1874–1965

Garry Wills cites the Latinate title of America's oldest Church music journal as evidence of the Latin prejudice of the pre-Vatican II Catholic intellectual. Having always had trouble spelling it properly in any language without a monstrous share of doodling, I submit that it is rather a transliteration of the umlaut in the German *Cäcilien-Verein* from which it immediately derived; from which it also earned a German stigma which it could never entirely doff through Swiss, Walloon, French, and Luxembourger editorships, and a long, benign Irish proprietorship.

John Baptist Singenberger had journeyed from his native Switzerland to Regensburg, Bavaria, in 1872 to make the acquaintance of Franz Xavier Witt, Franz Xavier Haberl, and the rest. By 1874, he had launched his American review as the official journal of an American *Cäcilien-Verein* established the year before. Witt's European counterpart dated only from 1867, and separate foundations followed in Ireland, Vienna, Italy, Bohemia, Moravia, Slavonia, and Belgium between 1878 and 1881. Pius IX's brief of December 16, 1870, *Multum ad Movendos Animos,* gave the original private organization the status of a papal association, the matter having been presented to the beleaguered pontiff during the sessions of Vatican I by bishops who were guardians of the several diocesan branches. It was a ploy which adumbrated the genesis of the CIMS from the Cäcilien Society for German Speaking Peoples (ACV) around the time of Vatican II.

The brief confirmed existing statutes, provided the movement with a cardinal protector as final overseer, and set forth principles and goals that germinated numerous future papal documents. While Pius IX had been properly circumspect in limiting the Medicean chant printing privilege of Pustet to thirty years, laws and statutes of the brief were made irrevocable and given "the eternal power of our approval." The same affirmation was tendered the American society in February of 1876, but for all that it wore this papal panoply, it never achieved Catholic universality.

While the early issues of the magazine were mostly German, with occasional articles and notices in English, and would remain so until as late as 1925, when Volume 52 appeared as the first issue entirely in English, Singenberger made two separate attempts to break the movement out of its Germanic shell. From 1882 to 1884, he published a monthly journal called *The Echo,* and from 1905 to 1906, the *Review of Church Music.* The first was put out by Pustet in New York, the second by himself in St. Francis, Wisconsin.

Both projects failed for lack of subscribers, and the good man must have blinked a bit when, in a supportive letter for the *Review of Church Music,* Bishop Maes of Covington wrote: "I have no doubt that your *Review of Church Music* will be a success. The reasons for my belief are: 1st, that you are now defending *not individual ideas to which many with some show of reason objected* [italics added], but a well-defined cause upon which all Church authorities agree, and principles reduced to practice by the Pope himself. 2nd, that you pledge yourself to edit the *Review* in strict conformity with the *Motu Proprio* of our Holy Father, Pius X." One surmises that he would have liked to respond in much the same manner as Monsignor John A. Ryan when accused of being a New Dealer. He is reported to have said: "Before the New Deal was, I am." As a matter of fact, it appears that with the promulgation of the *motu proprio,* Singenberger considered the work of the Cecilian Society to have been not only vindicated but finished. For there were no further annual conventions or election of officers. *Roma locuta, causa finita.* I do not know that any of those objecting "with some show of reason" played any part in the launching of the St. Gregory Society and its *Catholic Choirmaster* in 1915. The continued use of German in *Caecilia* probably did, for World War I was already in progress; and there were likely regional differences, although Singenberger had early support in the East, and J. Fischer & Bro., a factotum of the new society, had been his original publisher, both in Dayton, Ohio, and in New York City.

It appears that there were other problems contingent on the propagation and interpretation of the *motu proprio,* and perhaps matters of personality. In 1954, about the time we were trying to revitalize the old society, Casper Koch, a son-in-law of Singenberger and dean of Pittsburgh organists, wrote: "I refused to join the Society of St. Gregory. While I cannot go into details which prompted my decision, I may say that the circular inviting membership contained a dastardly attack on the St. Cecilia Society and, by implication, on Singenberger." As time went on, there was a good deal of line-crossing in the two organizations. But in the Church of the Sacred Heart in Pittsburgh, built by a notable Irish pastor, Singenberger is ensconced in a stained glass sanctuary window, and in a frieze on the opposite wall Carlo Rossini of the Society of St. Gregory is depicted as being pronged straight into the fires of hell by Satan himself.

Although one may read, for example, that Thomas Jefferson was wont to drop into the Catholic church in Philadelphia on occasion because "of the beauty of its music," Catholic Church music matters in the United States prior to Singenberger's journal are difficult to document. With the establishment of *Caecilia,* a picture emerges; and the thing that strikes one who peruses its pages most forcibly is their sameness. Not any kind of dullness, but the equivalency of all times: the same ideals, the same frustrations, the same impoverishment,[1] the same seeking after official shelter. By 1876, the journal had the approbation of Archbishop McCloskey of New York, James Roosevelt Bailey of Baltimore, Purcell of Cincinnati, Kenrick of St. Louis, Henni of Milwaukee, and a good many others from St. Paul to Buffalo. If there was no enthusiasm to the West, it is probably because there wasn't anything to speak of out there. The old missions, which once boasted a sizable body of their own music, were then silent and Lamy was just beginning his prolonged battle to establish his claim to all of the see of Santa Fe.

Documents printed and explained read much as they would for nearly a hundred years. "Religious Music" was hedged in by the privileged trio of chant, polyphony, and "suitable contemporary composition." Sacred songs which are customarily sung by the people during certain devotions "may be tolerated as far as the canon laws permit." There were vigorous nods to the needs of small churches and the proper employment of "the organ and other musical instruments." And long after it had become the fashion to berate the Cecilian movement, Father Vitry, after studying the most vital years of the magazine, adjudged that the total thrust then was something more than we had been able to muster since. Any historian of American Church music can tell you who John Singenberger was, as any musicologist can speak of Proske and Haberl.

There was heated discussion about the chant in 1876, and a contributor submitted this wild story about the genesis of the Medicean-Ratisbon edition of it: About a year prior to the opening of the First Vatican Council, the rector of the Propaganda College in Rome, one Don Loreto Jacovacci, circularized the bishops of the world in the interest of (a) a uniform grammar of plainchant, and (b) a new and corrected edition of all the chant books, said edition to be edited according to the Roman Medicean exemplar of the years 1614 and 1615. New offices were to be added, and upon acceptance and approval by the Holy See, its use was to be made obligatory in all cathedral and collegiate churches of the Latin rite. Several replies to the circular came to the attention of Father Francis Haberl of the Diocese of Passau, then in Rome as the chaplain and choirmaster of the German Church of Santa Maria dell'Anima. He immediately made Jacovacci's acquaintance, approving, as he did, of the proposals. Shortly thereafter, he had a letter from Pustet of Ratisbon telling him that someone in Rome had written about a manuscript of the Antiphonary and *Graduale* which was for sale, and which was about to be approved by the Sacred Congregation of Rites and made obligatory. Would Haberl check it out at this particular address? He found there the sister of a lately deceased Monsignor Alfieri, who had inherited eight folio volumes for which she expected 12,000 *scudi*, about 2,000 pounds sterling. One volume was written entirely in the modern bass clef, another in the tenor, a third with promiscuous sharps and flats, a fourth in white open notation, another divided into measured time bars, and so on. During Alfieri's lifetime, the Sacred Congregation of Rites had appointed a commission which was to report on his work. It had delayed its testimony as to its utter uselessness, but Haberl found that it had laid down a set of worthy principles in the event that such a project be undertaken, and had indicated the Medicean edition as a basis and norm.

Thus did Haberl conceive the idea of a new edition of the choral books, one which would correct the serious alterations in those purporting to be reproductions of the Medicean issued in Rome under Paul V, and one which would remedy the incompleteness of that issue, nothing more than the Graduale having ever appeared. Haberl told Pustet all he had seen and heard, and Pustet asked Haberl to learn, if he could, what conditions the Congregation would impose on editor and publisher of an official Graduale, and if a privilege might be obtained.

There was a verbal reply to the effect that, if Pustet would undertake, at his own risk, to reprint the Medicea under the supervision of a commission named by the Holy Father, to bring it out in as clear or clearer type than the original, and to provide and print Gregorian chant for all the festivals authorized since 1615, he would obtain a privilege of thirty years.

It looked like a proper enterprise to Pustet. He asked Haberl to undertake the transcription of the music, along with the matter of supplying music for the new feasts, and obtained a favorable reply to a formal petition from the SRC on October 1, 1868. Later, since the immense cost of an edition in folio would render his thirty-year privilege pretty useless, he obtained the right to issue an octavo or manual edition.[2]

For all the initiative of Haberl and Pustet, it is clear from the rescripts that it was considered no mere private endeavor. The edition was to be scrutinized by a commission already deputized, and it would not be published until it was pronounced *ad instar Mediceae.* Though it would forever labor under such accusations, it was of no diocesan or national design, but an official Roman one, with all the *nihil contrariis obstantibus* trappings that were the earmark of the Congregation of Rites. When the first sheet was printed, Haberl and Pustet were presented to Pius IX. It is said that he took the magnificent piece of printing in hand and began singing (as he *could* sing) the Asperges Me. Then he expressed his satisfaction that nothing had been altered!

Arguments raged throughout the Catholic world much as they would about the Editio Vaticana forty years later. And they were pretty much the same: everybody was promoting his own effort. The Abbé Bonhoume wrote that the Ratisbon edition, superb as it was and obviously under powerful patronage, had one fault—it had come too late. After the Gallican return to the Roman Liturgy, France was divided into two camps, those who accepted the truncated chant of the sixteenth and seventeenth centuries, and those who opted for the more ancient basis of Rheims-Cambrai. The Malines edition of 1848 claimed that, besides having all the Roman virtues, its Ordinaries were Antwerpian. Père Lambillotte, S.J., long before Solesmes was ever reestablished, had operated on the principle of reducing chant to its original sobriety. The carom of each diocesan edition was, however, to claim direct lineage from St. Gregory.[3]

Haberl admitted that the Ratisbon book had modifications, but it was not claimed that Palestrina made them, and he specifically declared that while the Medicean did not always faithfully reproduce the original manuscripts, "it never departed from the spirit of Gregorian song or omitted its peculiar characteristics." I remember Father Vitry, an adamant adherent to the *Vaticana* of 1905, remarking that the old chant, like that of Mechelen and Ratisbon, couldn't have been all that bad, since he had been brought up on it. It was musicologically indefensible, but the musicological aspects of chant were not far advanced, and the basic plea was not only for an aesthetic or scientific norm, but for the guarantee of a universally acceptable official song. With more aesthetics and more science, the same plea would be made for the *Vaticana*. The fight has been going on for a long time, and will probably continue. When *Caecilia* undertook during the 1950s to restate Peter Wagner's defense of the Vatican edition as against the aesthetic and pseudoscience of neo-Solesmes, it was sometimes incredibly accused of defending Haberl's *Medicea.*

Singenberger's *Chant Manual* followed closely the *Magister Choralis* of Haberl, but he was ready for the *Vaticana* when it came, having preferred for some years previously the chant manner of the monks of Beuron. He kept to the official Vatican line against the proponents of the new Solesmes or American mensuralists like Father Bonvin. And he continued to report the peaks, the valleys, and the foibles.

Long before Father Finn, Father Young had an enthusiastic following at the Paulist Church on Fifty-ninth Street. For Mass and Vespers it was Gregorian, but his St. Cecilia Chorus of twenty-six young men and thirty boys descended to "harmonized chorales" and even glees. The Palestrina Society of Suspension Bridge, Niagara County, New York, might be justly proud of its wares, but Singenberger winced at the announcement of an Eastern church for the "First Sunday of Advent within the octave of St. Cecilia: *Gloria in Excelsis, Salve Regina,* Closing Overture—Rossini." Ads for different makes of the melodeon and harmonium foreshadowed those for electronics a century later, music lists read like the St. Gregory White List and "educational" materials like a page out of *Musart.*[4]

Felix Mendelssohn was reported to have written to his dear sister, Rebecca, of the dreadful music at Mass in Düsseldorf, where there was *"nichts von älteren Italienen."* He had better luck in Bonn and Cologne where he heard six Masses of Palestrina, some Allegri, Baini, Lassus, and Pergolesi. He propounded what he would do about it if he were a Catholic.

In the United States, Archbishop Kenrick had said in his *Moral Theology* that it was acceptable to sing the *Veni Sancte Spiritus* before the sermon. Holy Name Cathedral in Chicago was dedicated to the strains of Gregorian, the "graceful and charming Mass" by Greith, faux bourdon responses, and the *Veni* of Brosig ("perhaps the *lightest* thing we sing"), and the finale of Beethoven's *Fifth.* "Photographs" of Palestrina, Josquin, and Willaert were modestly priced, and it was clear, as someone in Barnard's *Musical Monthly* had remarked, that Haydn, Mozart, and Beethoven had been driven out of their own Church.

W. F. M. of St. Paul blasted the choirs and composers of the time: "The Proper parts are entirely ignored, while the Kyrie, Gloria, etc., are brought out in a carnival of harmony. . . . Where are the minds of the congregation during the Offertory, *the solemnest part of the Mass,* (on the collection maybe?) while their favorite prima donna disgorges some heartrending solo? . . . If she can trill or force a hiccough the effect will be positively sublime. If the listener has happened to hear her solo at the opera, the vision of ballet dancers would be difficult to describe. He is just ready to break into loud applause when the striking of the gong reminds him that he is in Church." The gongs are gone, but not much else. W. F. M. adjudged that only the Church of the Assumption could pass muster in that city, and it only partially.

Diocesan Cecilian societies traveled to Cleveland and Detroit to concertize each other, and their presidents had to be approved by the bishop. Congregational singing was one of the objects listed in the constitution and bylaws. The coming Chant Congress at Strasbourg—where Peter Wagner would argue that, archeology aside, the Church after a lapse of 250 years had a representative, universally official chant—was detailed in a 1905 issue of the *Review of Church Music.* Persons to attend were listed, and though all factions seemed to be represented, it was felt that the papal commission was largely composed of adherents of the Solesmes system. Be that as it may, Pothier, later sent off to St. Wandrille and other distant ports, and Wagner eventually, if only officially, won the battle; had indeed by a direct intervention of Pius X already won it.

One doesn't imagine that a signed article in a 1906 *Review,* entitled "The *Motu Proprio* on Long Island," won it many friends. It panned everything going on there, particularly the Lambillotte Ave Maria which had been rendered feelingly during the Offertory by Messrs. Mates and McKnight of the Castle Square Opera Company. One Joseph Otten was particularly disturbed because Rosewig, frequently sung, was a Jew and therefore a desecration of the temple. He also berated Madame Schumann-Heink for playing in a musical comedy. Singenberger debunked an announcement in an Ohio newspaper to the effect that the Vatican edition of Gregorian chant, edited by

Don Perosi from manuscripts discovered in the Abbey of Monte Cassino, had arrived in this country, for none of the ten-odd authorized publishers had as yet received advance sheets.

My own connection with *Caecilia* was but an echo of all that vitality. It is memorable chiefly for friends and enemies made, the collaboration of notable scholars and practitioners, and financial help given. At one point, our attorney and acting financial secretary suggested that we try to find a hundred people who considered the project worth an investment of a hundred dollars. He said he did, and by God there ought to be ninety-nine others around who knew more about it than himself. There were, but not all had a hundred dollars. It was kept going pretty much through gifts of individual and choir members and the facilities and personnel proffered by Monsignor Wegner, Director of Boys Town.

In the end, we managed to pay off a $2,000 loan, and contribute a like amount as our share of the merger with the St. Gregory Society. The CMAA venture, had it worked, would probably have been our best contribution. I soon learned what Arthur Reilly meant when, on turning the magazine back to the Society of St. Cecilia, he said: "You can see where I was getting off at." All he asked was that, in deference to the memory of Singenberger, we furnish a five-year guarantee of not turning it over to another group.

I had been a little too harsh in describing the two Catholic Church music magazines as mere publishers' journals. Who else was interested, and who, like me, imagined that we could manage without compromising advertising? The gesture toward reestablishing the American Society of St. Cecilia was mostly just that, despite the new Nebraska incorporation, and the spiritual privilege renewed by Pope John. But we had reason to be proud of the integrity of our contributors. Our correspondent in Italy refused to do a musical autopsy of Perosi because he couldn't think of anything good to say about him. There is not much in Volumes 83–92 that I am now ashamed of, except bad spelling and bad proofreading. It's all there, and I entertain no illusions about anyone being interested enough to look through it. Nor any illusions about a second spring. At my age one looks forward not to a second spring, but just any spring.

NOTES

Chapter I

1. Tradition is the handing down of many things; but of what are usually called musical traditions, Paul Hindemith has written that there is no such thing, only competence.

2. Dom Lambert Beauduin (1873–1960), was a Belgian Benedictine of the Abbey of Mont César, Louvain. He is generally credited with being one of the initiators of the twentieth-century liturgical movement.

3. L. Bouyer, *The Liturgy Revived*, Notre Dame University Press, 1964.

Chapter II

1. This is perhaps an idea harking back to St. Augustine's treatise on free will, in which he held that because art could be used badly it could not be a virtue. St. Thomas (*Summa Theologica*, 1–11, q. 57, a. 3) argued on the contrary that art was a virtue or habit of the speculative order, that it was a good and an end in itself. Further, that the matter of its use was proper to the appetitive virtue (prudence), and that indeed a good and proper use was not possible unless it was art (*"quamvis bonus usus sine arte esse non possit"*). In none of the documents which touched upon sacred music do I recall any trespass upon the wisdom of Thomas Aquinas, though, heaven knows, he was used for everything else. When one was trying to make the point that sacred music must in some manner be intrinsically holy, the *Summa* was perhaps dangerous ground. It remained for Paul VI to point directly to the Angelic Doctor. In July of 1976, Pope Paul addressed the participants in a seminar on the influence of religious inspiration in American art: "But we are convinced that today, too, the work of art, not sacrificing anything of the just autonomy to which it is entitled and which St.

Thomas already recognized . . . is a potential vehicle of a religious message."

Neither art nor the speculative faculty make a work good as to its use; its use indeed may be determined by extraneous laws, but the laws of that use will not govern the confection of the work of art. Thus the Church quite properly may govern the use of art in her liturgy. But one of the end results of some of her legislation, intended or not, turned out to be a ban on whole segments of musical art, not because they were "profane or lascivious," for they clearly were not, but almost, it seemed, because they were monumental *bona facta* in themselves. This is not to deny the propriety of cautioning against certain qualities of ornateness, length, and repetitiveness, which may or may not have hindered the "liturgical flow." It is to assert that it set whole schools of contrivers to churning out music, not according to the principles of art but according to the extraneous principles of its use. So that in the end there was little art and less use.

2. These are probably best epitomized in the *motu proprio* on sacred music of Pope St. Pius X. (November 22, 1903). He insisted that "it [sacred music] must be true art. In no other way can it affect the minds of the hearers in the manner in which the church intends in admitting into the liturgy the art of sound."

3. B. H. F. Hellebusch published his *Katholische Gesang und Gebetbuch* in New York in 1858. It typified the compilations of superficial service music then appearing in almost every language and every land. A century later most Church musicians would consider them laughable, and assert that the Church was fairly rid of such like; but Hellebusch and his cohorts, it would appear, have the last laugh.

4. It is all right to say that art must be ordered toward man's final end. But so must everything else, including speculative virtue, or knowledge. Art, as St. Thomas says, has nothing to do with morality. The negative moralism of the official pronouncements appears evenly pronounced right up until the end. Thus, in *Musicae Sacrae Disciplina* (1955): "The church must insist that this art remain within its proper limits. . . . Trent forbids those musical works in which something lascivious or impure is mixed with organ music or singing . . . illicit and immoderate elements which had arrogantly been inserted into sacred music. . . . It is a question which is not to be answered by an appeal to the principles of art and aesthetics . . . art and works of art must be *judged* [italics added] in the light of their conformity and concord with man's last end. . . . Some people wrongly assert that art should be entirely exempted from every rule which does not spring from art itself. . . . The out-worn dictum 'art for art's sake' entirely neglects the end for which every creature is made." By association it might, but not in itself. It simply doesn't go into the matter.

And in the 1958 Instruction of the Congregation of Rites on Sacred Music and the Sacred Liturgy: "The works of sacred polyphony of ancient or recent composers must not be allowed in liturgical functions before it is first of all ascertained that they are composed or adapted in such a way as to correspond to the norms and admonitions set forth in *Musicae Sacrae Discplinia."* The same was to hold *a fortiori,* for "compositions of modern sacred music." And when in doubt? Consult the diocesan commission—the end-setter of ends! One wonders how the compositions in question have earned the appellative "sacred" before they have been judged. It is not a matter of faulty translation, although those provided by the National Catholic Welfare Conference (NCWC) News Service are not without some first class blunders. As when it had Pius XII saying, in *Musicae Sacrae Disciplina:* "It [Georgian chant] attained new beauty in almost all parts of Christian Europe after the eighth or ninth century because of its accompaniment by a new musical instrument called the 'organ.' " What it said was that Gregorian chant "was not the only means in the eighth and ninth centuries by which . . . new splendour was being added to worship, inasmuch as the use in churches of the musical instrument called the organ had already begun." (Even Franz Witt, one of the progenitors of the Cecilian movement, had said in the Foreword to his chant accompaniments that, while he hotly defended the principles upon which they were based, they were nonetheless evil. The trouble was that he must have considered them a necessary evil or he wouldn't have fooled with them.)

One might, with some show of benevolence, understand the intended thrust of all such statements as the above, and it would be an enlightening exercise to measure what passes as Church music today against them. Unfortunately, an overall picture emerges, and it is neither rationally acceptable nor pleasant: that of the Church as schoolmaster, ruler in hand, ready to rap the knuckles of deviant artists.

5. Rudolf Graber, "Religion and Art," in *Sacred Music and Liturgy Reform,* North Central Publishing Company, St. Paul, Minnesota, 1969. [Italics added.]

6. Johann Michael Sailer (1751–1834) was, like Graber, the bishop of Regensburg. As professor of theology at the University of Landshut, in 1808, he gave an address to faculty and students on "The Alliance between Art and Religion."

Chapter III

1. Father Vitry was a Benedictine of the Abbey of Maredsous, Belgium. He had studied theology under Dom Columba Marmion and music under Edgar Tinel at the Lemmensinstituut in Malines, and also in Brussels when, around 1910, Tinel became the director of the conservatory there. He came to the United States in 1925 at the persuasion of Dom Virgil Michel of St. John's Abbey in Collegeville, Minnesota, who was then about the business of launching a vigorous liturgical movement in the United States. Father Vitry became an associate edi-

tor of *Orate Fratres* (now *Worship*), and edited *Caecilia* from 1941 until 1950. He worked at music education throughout the Midwest and West, and in later years found a home at the motherhouse of the Sister of the Precious Blood in O'Fallon, Missouri, where he established a chant school and a modest press which he called Fides Jubiians. The state of Church music, however, never gave him much to be jubilant about. Wearily listing his disappointments over what he heard in Europe on his last trip to Belgium, he wrote: "I might just as well fight in your company. . . . They should know better, but they don't."

2. The term is used to distinguish the followers of Dom Mocquereau from the earlier "oratorical" Solesmes school of Dom Pothier. The former held an inexorable law according to which all rhythm was reducible to twos and threes. The *ictus,* an accent which miraculously was not an accent, must be binary or ternary whether one counted from the beginning or the end of the phrase and regardless of what syllable it might or might not hit. Dr. Eugene Selhorst of Eastman used to characterize the *ictus* as "the little man who wasn't there." And Terence Gahagan, a onetime wag about Westminster during the days of Richard Terry, would ask: "How can you 'uplift' an accented syllable when you are singing it, as suggested by Solesmes. . . . Do you rise on tiptoe, raise your eyebrows, swing an arm upwards?"

3. Arthur Lourie, "De la Melodie," *La Vie intellectuelle,* 1936.

4. White had sent on reams of experimental Englished material that he had used during his tenure at St. Mary the Virgin in New York. And in June, 1968, Sowerby wrote to me: "It would help to improve the standards of music in both our Churches if we could use virtually the same music, whether it be composed to English or Latin texts. The Roman Church would profit by having available a complete and magnificent repertory of music of the highest standard, and new to it, and as a result could begin to discard many of the Masses and other music of questionable value and by second-rate composers, which have, unfortunately, been the standard fare in many places."

5. Monsignor Overath was president of the papal International Consociato of Sacred Music at the time. He had long been a force in sacred music matters in German-speaking countries and, indeed, in Rome.

6. Christopher Dawson, *Religion and the Rise of Western Culture,* Doubleday, 1958.

7. Walter Buszin, retired professor of Liturgics at Concordia Seminary, St. Louis, Missouri, had been editor of *Response.*

Chapter IV

1. This was an apostolic constitution on promoting the study of Latin. Promulgated on February 22, 1962, it came as something of a bombshell, for it "established and ordered that both bishops and superiors general of religious orders . . . see to it with paternal concern

that none of their subjects, moved by an inordinate desire for novelty, writes against the use of Latin either in the teaching of the sacred discplines or in the sacred rites of the liturgy." Latin, of course, was widely held to be the chief barrier to *participatio,* and it was the first to come crashing down a few years later. Thereafter, that magic and overworked noun was invoked to admit every sort of inanity, to destroy any tradition, no matter how substantive, that did not curry to its salvific intercession. Somewhere beneath all that imbroglio there lay a hidden desire not so much to participate as to pontificate.

2. Louise Cuyler, to the author.

3. Nicholas Jacques Lemmens had been a professional organist with no particular Church music background. Late in life, he cajoled Belgian authorities into letting him found a Church music institute; and when he died, quipped one of his successors, "the bishops were stuck with it."

4. For that matter, the Church's opposition to instruments other than the organ is nearly as old as recorded musical history. Though instrumentalists were periodically expelled from the Church, they always returned in short order, and were welcomed by the lower clergy.

5. K. G. Fellerer, *The History of Catholic Church Music,* Helicon Press, 1961.

6. Parody not to be taken in the pejorative sense of burlesque. The parody Mass was one structured, sometimes inimitably, on the tunes of secular texts.

7. *Sacred Music,* vol. 93, no. 1.

8. I could cite a thousand contrarieties to that assumption among young and old, or middleaged—like Heywood Broun. One of the few reasons his stunned friends could adduce for the old scoffer's joining the Church was the appeal of its liturgy.

Chapter V

1. As far as the Church was concerned, its very own school system, begot at such sacrifice, had not been all that much help in providing its music, excepting the usual children's choir. But there was little carryover to secondary level, parish choir, and/or congregation. In the Midwest, at least, one of the crazier statutes forbade nuns, the likely parish musicians, to conduct any male past the age of puberty. We were better off when John Singenberger's Normal School in Milwaukee was turning out lay organists. They were now clinging to a few scattered church jobs, running bebop record shops on the side to make a living, and slipping out for a beer between the *O Salutaris* and *Tantum Ergo* to ponder what might have been.

2. Moe is not an organization call letter nor any kind of generic term. Moe is Frank D. Szynskie, my unfailing associate and successor. The "D" is for Darwin. It was suggested that he change that to Francis ten minutes before Father Flanagan baptized him.

3. A canon law-oriented pastor, for example, would not allow his

organist to play the piano at the home funeral of a neighbor. I was quietly but officially warned about a concert my boys had given in a Baptist church. And the Milwaukee chancery all but boycotted a concert there, because we were being sponsored by the Sertoma Club, and the proceeds were to go for swimming scholarships at the YMCA.

4. Father Francis Brunner, C.Ss.R., an indefatigable idealist, had translated Jungmann's *Mass of the Roman Rite* before many knew who Jungmann was. He later Englished Fellerer's *History of Catholic Church Music*. Monsignor Schuler is the current editor of *Sacred Music*.

5. Arthur Reilly kept the magazine going as a kind of trust from old John Singenberger.

6. A priest of the Italian Congregation of the Missionaries of St. Charles, Father Rossini was the oracle in matters of Church music in Pittsburgh. With the backing of Bishop Boyle, he frequently placed clerical violators of his interpretation of the law on a blacklist published in the diocesan paper. After serving a stint with the Italian Society of St. Caecilia during the 1950 Holy Year, he was no longer welcome in Pittsburgh. He remained in Italy, where he puts the royalties of his not inconsiderable number of publications to work building and supporting an Italian Boys Town. No set of footnotes can do justice to the patriarchal characters of that lost establishment of Church musicians. I should like some time to gather a Festshrift for them, for they were seldom fested, often shrifted.

7. There was only this official relaxation by the time of Pius XII's *Musicae Sacrae Disciplina* (1955): "Where boy singers are not available in sufficient number, it is permitted that a choir of men and women or girls may sing the liturgical texts during solemn mass in a place destined for this sole purpose outside the sanctuary, provided that the men are entirely separated from the women and girls and that anything unseemly be avoided."

8. In *Bibel und Liturgie* 37, 1963–64, pp. 248–49.

9. The Liturgical Conference, Washington, D.C., 1967. It amplified considerably the original publication of the Kansas City papers which were called "Harmony and Discord: An Open Forum on Church Music."

10. The Composers' Forum for Catholic Worship, originally a composition committee within the framework of the CMAA.

11. An international association for the retention and promotion of the Latin Mass.

12. Romita was the accepted canonist of Church music law, and is an official of Pueri Cantores.

13. George Devine, *Liturgical Renewal: An Agonizing Reappraisal*, Alba House, New York, 1973.

14. CIMS Rome, 1969; American edition: Northcentral Publishing Co., St. Paul, Minnesota.

15. A notable guest was Dom Anselm Hughes, the Anglican Benedictine chant scholar. Some years before, I had reprinted and propa-

gated as best I could the English Medieval and Plain-Song Society's translation of the Preface to the Vatican Gradual, quite properly called "An Explanation of the Vatican Chant." From the point of view of both language and clarity, it was superior to our official translation, and in its treatment of the rhythmic quality of the *virga* in melismas, it was less enigmatic than the Latin original. Dom Anselm had done that translation some sixty years earlier, and, expressing mild surprise at its still being circulated, asked if he might have a copy of his own work.

16. As late as the spring of 1976, a midwest archbishop told the public press that the pope had *ordered* Mass to be said in English, and that any Latin liturgy needed specific authorization from his chancery!

17. And all of the national diversification, of course, decimates the available number of "competent composers." No one country gave us Dunstable, Josquin, Lassus, Palestrina, Byrd, and Victoria—or the patrimony of Gregorian.

Chapter VI

1. There were certainly seeds of ambivalence in the Constitution itself. Anent the chant, for example, just what did "all things being equal" and "pride of place" really mean? The *Kyriale Simplex*, with which the CIMS had been involved, hardly represents any pride of place; and the *Graduale Simplex*, which had not been its suggestion, and in whose formation it played no part, was a feint that would have put the traditional chant in anything but pride of place had the early urgency for a specific framework of Propers persisted. It was, in fact, a latter-day version of the *Graduale Pauperum*, although I have the impression that this term more aptly describes authentic seasonal chants—like those contained in the eighteenth-century *Extractus Responsorii*, a book gotten out for smaller congregations in the Diocese of Mainz—than the truncated nightmare which is the *Graduale Simplex*. (Eric Werner was close to the truth when he declared publicly, as no Catholic was willing to, that the Church had abandoned its chant.)

2. The old business of voting members: when I inquired whether there was any sense in my going to Rome for a *coetus de re musica* of the consilium, I was told yes, and that I would have a "consultative" vote. The consultative vote was exactly the kind one gets from Lou Harris or George Gallup, although for what it is worth, I sometimes imagined that I recognized an echo of my own thought or language in one or the other redaction.

3. Father Annibale Bugnini was secretary to the Consilium. Speaking at an Italian liturgical convention in 1968, he airily described the first four years of the Consilium's history as "four years of musical polemics." He is now the archbishop of a Near East see, and liturgists commonly think that he has been exiled.

4. Likewise, they hadn't the courage to take up Overath's challenge

to interdict polyphony outright if they sincerely considered it in conflict with *participatio actuosa.* Instead, in Draft I, the suggestion was made that polyphonic offerings be selected on the basis of concentus. I pointed out that this could only be interpreted as signifying that rash of compositions—especially since about 1958—for "schola and people," which had precious little to do with the *thesaurus* everybody was talking about, and certainly would not be taken for a mandated revival of the few genuine articles like the several Masses of Isaac or the *Missa in Festis Apostolorum II* of Palestrina, which likely hadn't envisioned a congregation joining anyway.

5. ". . . and we don't want grand opera, do we?" They meant, of course, that it had been grand opera all along, so flat their taste. Nothing grand, opera or no, did we get, but burlesque.

6. In about 1950, the Vatican had declared Rotary Clubs off-limits to Canadian Catholics.

7. On Ascension Day of 1964, Paul VI said, ". . . not only have the artists abandoned the Church, but Mother Church has also let down the artists . . . limited her outlook too much with all kinds of rigid rules . . . and finally took to substitutes, to downright trash."

8. *Notitiae,* a journal of commentary on announcements and studies of matters liturgical, issued monthly by the Vatican Press.

Chapter VII

1. The German practice of singing vernacular approximations of liturgical texts at Mass.

2. An attempt to employ the Anglican solution here, and put it some place in the Communion and Dismissal rites, had failed.

3. "The Church Musician," in *Concilium* 72: *Liturgy: Self-Expression of the Church,* ed. by Herman Schmidt, Herder and Herder, New York, 1972.

4. Ibid.

5. Why should they be subjected to fifth-rate rock there, when they can tune in to the real thing on their transistors once they are in the vestibule?

Chapter VIII

1. The Rt. Rev. Urbanus Bomm, O.S.B., sometime abbot of Maria Laach. See P. Dominicus Johner, O.S.B., *Wort und Ton im Choral,* Breitkopf & Härtel, Leipzig, 1953.

2. It is true that St. Jerome eschewed the classical polish of his early years when he came to translating the Scriptures. That was partially because too great a divergence from then current readings would have been unacceptable—and nearly was—to clergy and laity alike. His gigantic effort, textual corrections included, would have gone for

naught. It is not uncommon nowadays to write off Jerome (and Erasmus) as mere philologists who lacked the modern tools of criticism. But what he accomplished was a great reading in a new and vibrant tongue; far from assimilating the vulgar Latin, he all but demolished it. The critical acumen of present-day translators is not at issue. Their seeming crassness in matters literary is. It is difficult to imagine their labors engendering centuries of mission, or music. See J. N. D. Kelly, *Jerome* (Harper & Row, 1975): " . . . his [Jerome's] Old Testament raised the vulgar Latinity of Christians to the heights of great literature."

3. Joseph Connelly, *Hymns of the Roman Liturgy*, Newman Press, 1957.

4. Said to have been instigated by Cardinal Bea in the interest of a classical realignment. In many areas, it rendered impossible the singing, or even common recitation, not just of the psalter but of oft-used canticles like the Benedictus and Magnificat, because one used one book, one the other. As far back as the time the Gallican psalter replaced the Roman, the song texts were left intact, and are still retained in the Vatican Gradual, even though at times they differ from the missal. It is also said that neither of several revisions that Jerome made of his Vulgate psalter attained common usage because it was too late to tinker with the liturgical books.

5. Dare one mention the sometimes tenuous kinship between the three readings, which many people feel only a professional Scripture scholar can detect? Most homilists have all they can do to be homilists, and may well turn out to be exponents of the ancient allegorical school or Origen, rather than modern interpreters of writ.

6. What is one to say about the great Proper antiphons of morning and evening prayer? On the thirtieth Sunday of the year, Cycle B, for example, the Gospel tells of the healing of the blind Bartimaeus, and the antiphon for the Magnificat has the publican going down to his house justified.

7. *An Index of Gregorian Chant*, vol. I (Alphabetical), vol. II (Thematic), Harvard University Press, 1969. Also *Ordo Cantus Missae*, Vatican Press. The new Solesmes *Graduale* follows this *Ordo*.

8. Charles Dreisoerner, St. Mary's University, San Antonio, Texas, in *Sacred Music*, vol. 97, no. 3, Fall 1970. Father Dreisoerner, S.M., studied with Peter Wagner, Karl Fellerer, and Joseph Gogniat at the University of Fribourg, Switzerland. His *The Psychology of Liturgical Music* (1945) was published by the Maryhurst Press, Kirkwood, Missouri. He remarked further, and rightly, that "such multiple shifts of parts—makes any adaptation to any Latin Masses impossible." That would include the simplest Gregorian Gloria.

9. I am aware, of course, that the musical text in the missal and most missalettes is an approximation of the old ferial chant tone. No matter. Whoever sang a Preface—and those who sing it in the vernacular today—instinctively opted for the naturally rising nomenclature over "lift."

10. Cardinal Carberry had said that the translation was an interim one. Father Dreisoerner's intervention to the CMAA was futile, as might have been expected. But the Lutherans, on page 9 of their *Worship Supplement* (red book) had already rejected it.

11. They no longer receive even a dribble of royalties, and don't even know whether their publishers still exist. When, if ever, they do write for the Church again, it will be for cash on delivery.

12. Since these lines were written, FEL has brought suit against the Archdiocese of Chicago and five parishes there for violation of copyright. FEL is right, of course. Anyone with little enough taste to pirate their materials deserves to be sued.

Chapter IX

1. The first official Roman Catholic International Congress on the Liturgy to which the laity were invited. I have remarked elsewhere that that was not the way Father Vitry saw it.

2. I count it, by now, an authentic experience that Gregorian was pervasive beyond any expectation. A nonrhythmic, modal pointing of vernacular texts works—even for very large congregations.

3. Monsignor Rigaud, bishop of Pamiers, signatory and vigorous promoter of the French hierarchy's directives.

Chapter X

1. There are these directions for "Lord, Receive this Company": "Whisper slowly into cupped hands, whisper slowly into open hands: standing with hands raised high . . . arms extended, arms lowered . . . clasp hands with person next to you. . . . Pause . . . whisper slowly, does not have to be together . . . whisper slowly into cupped hands . . . alternately. . . ."

2. *Erasmus and His Age,* ed. by Hans J. Hillerbrand, Harper & Row, 1970.

Chapter XI

1. In its first years, Westendorf's World Library of Sacred Music (WLSM) was engaged almost exclusively in importing sacred music from abroad.

2. Lorenzo Perosi was choirmaster at the Sistine Chapel, Licinio Refice at St. Mary Major. Both had published almost innumerable pieces of religious music.

3. Just what phenomena like *Godspell* and *Jesus Christ Superstar* are expected to do for the faith of the young is quite beyond me, though one might surmise that their frequent church-related productions expect them to do something. Malcolm Muggeridge has observed that the scenario for the latter was written by Ernest Renan rather more

than a century ago, but that even he would not be pleased with the finished product.

4. Francis Burgess, musical director of the Anglican Gregorian Association 1910–1948.

5. One such dimension which I have heard little discussed might be the composition of musical settings for the hymnic elements of the New Testament. These are clearly marked in many new editions, and used as such in the new breviary (Apoc. 15: 3–4; Col. 1:12–20, etc.).

6. Monsignor Haberl has moved from the presidency of the Regensburg Church Music School to that of the Pontifical Institute in Rome.

7. See her comprehensive article on the works of Langlais, *Musica Sacra,* February 1976.

8. The hour of Prime has been dropped from the Roman breviary. One of the other three is said as a "prayer during the day."

Chapter XII

1. Paul Henry Lang, "The *Patrimonium Musicae Sacrae* and the Task of Sacred Music Today," in *Sacred Music and Liturgy Reform,* North Central Publishing Company, St. Paul, Minnesota, 1969.

Appendix

1. Singenberger did have faith in ultimate solvency: he offered a thirty-year subscription for $25.50.

2. The withdrawal of this edition in favor of the new Editio Vaticana would occasion an understandable but regrettable last ditch defense, and Rome ultimately minced few words with Haberl.

3. It is related that in the year 787 Charlemagne was called upon to settle a fracas between the French and Italian singers during the Easter festivals in Rome. The French pretended to sing more agreeably than the Italians, who countered by accusing the French of corrupting, disfiguring, and despoiling the true chant which *they* had received from Pope Gregory. Charlemagne, in a classic case of presumption, is said to have ruled in favor of the Italians.

4. Journal of the National Catholic Music Educators Association.